MAGICAL CREATURES HANDBOOK

DIBUJAR CRIATURAS MÁGICAS | DISEGNARE LE CREATURE MAGICHE | DESENHAR CRIATURAS MÁGICAS

© 2009 **booQs** publishers bvba
Godefriduskaai 22
2000 Antwerp
Belgium
Tel.: +32 3 226 66 73
Fax: +32 3 226 53 65
www.booqs.be
info@booqs.be

ISBN: 978-94-60650-18-5
WD: D/2009/11978/019
(Q019)

Illustrations: Sergio Guinot Studio
Texts: Sergio Guinot Studio
Text edition: Cristian Campos
Art direction: Mireia Casanovas Soley
Layout: Maira Purman
Translation: Cillero & de Motta

Editorial project:

maomao publications
Via Laietana, 32, 4.º, of. 104
08003 Barcelona, Spain
Tel.: +34 932 688 088
Fax: +34 933 174 208
maomao@maomaopublications.com
www.maomaopublications.com

Printed in China

MAGICAL CREATURES HANDBOOK

DIBUJAR CRIATURAS MÁGICAS **|** DISEGNARE LE CREATURE MAGICHE **|** DESENHAR CRIATURAS MÁGICAS

booQs

CONTENTS

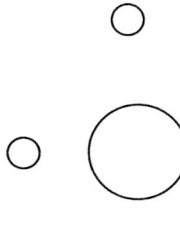

"Even a child could do it." How many times have we heard this phrase in a casual conversation on contemporary art? The same statement could easily apply to the creation of mythological and fantasy characters: at first it may not seem so difficult to design a creature similar to an orc, elf or dragon. However, anyone who has seen the process of designing an imaginary creature from scratch can testify that the task is a lot more complex than it first seems. Merely cutting out and copying pieces of the creatures from the major classical mythologies is not enough to achieve a character that makes sense (metaphorically speaking, as mythological creatures do not need to make sense). Not to mention the complexity of creating a mythological setting that is home to these creatures and which provides them with a perfectly balanced, natural space. A single incoherence in the planning could spoil the wonderful, complex and studied fantasy world.

This is not the only difficulty: the fantasy genre is inexplicably branded with a childish and superficial stigma. We say inexplicably because when it comes down to it literature from the dense,

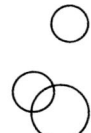

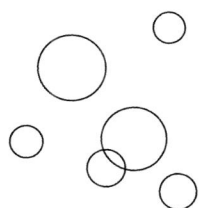

complex and baroque *Ulysses* by James Joyce to bestsellers, such as *The Da Vinci Code* are all fantasy literature.

Not even the realist novel can be considered as little more than fantasy with some true-to-life pretensions. And this poses a difficulty, because the genre is burdened with original sin that only can be redeemed by supposedly adult transcendence and arguments. Nevertheless, the fantasy genre is neither serious nor easy. It requires a playful and innocent spirit and the capacity to astonish that few adults hold on to post-adolescence.

This book, a true morphological catalogue aimed at comic book and illustration professionals, and also fantasy genre fans, compiles more than 500 characters that have mostly been designed from scratch. Conceived as a source of ideas for creators, some of those ideas being crazy while others more realistic, this volume is the essential handbook for all those who want to delve into the world of fantasy literature.

Sergio Guinot
www.artesecuencial.com

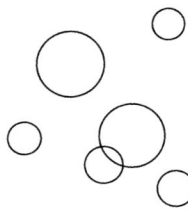

«Hasta un niño podría hacerlo». ¿Cuántas veces hemos oído esa frase en una conversación informal sobre arte contemporáneo? La misma afirmación podría aplicarse fácilmente a la creación de personajes fantásticos y mitológicos: a primera vista, no parece tan difícil diseñar una criatura similar a un orco, o a un elfo, o a un dragón. Sin embargo, y como podrá atestiguar cualquiera que se haya visto en el trance de diseñar una criatura fantástica desde cero, la tarea es bastante más complicada de lo que puede parecer en un principio. Y es que no basta con recortar y copiar «piezas» de las criaturas de las grandes mitologías clásicas para dar con un resultado que tenga pies y cabeza (metafóricamente hablando, por supuesto; en sentido estricto, las criaturas mitológicas no necesitan tener pies y cabeza). Por no hablar de lo complejo que resulta crear un marco mitológico que albergue a esas criaturas y les otorgue su espacio en un equilibrio natural perfectamente trabado. Una única incoherencia en el planteamiento puede echar a perder el mundo fantástico más rico, complejo y estudiado que podamos imaginar.

A esa primera dificultad se suma una segunda: el género fantástico carga, incomprensiblemente, con el estigma de «infantil» y «superficial». Decimos «incomprensiblemente» porque a fin de cuentas toda la literatura, desde el denso, intrincado y barroco *Ulises* de Joyce hasta *bestsellers* como *El código da Vinci*, son literatura fantástica.

Ni siquiera la llamada novela realista puede considerarse algo más que fantasía con pretensiones de verosimilitud. Y eso resulta ser una dificultad, porque carga al género con un pecado original que sólo puede ser redimido a base de trascendencia y argumentos supuestamente adultos.

No obstante, el género fantástico no es serio, aunque tampoco es fácil. Requiere de un espíritu juguetón y de la inocencia y la capacidad de asombro que sólo unos pocos adultos conservan una vez superada la adolescencia.

Este libro —un auténtico catálogo morfológico destinado a profesionales del cómic y la ilustración, pero también al aficionado al género fantástico— reúne más de 500 personajes diseñados, en su gran mayoría, desde cero. Concebido como una fuente de ideas para el creativo, algunas de ellas totalmente disparatadas y otras bastante cercanas a la verosimilitud, este volumen es un instrumento de consulta imprescindible para todo aquel que pretenda sumergirse en las procelosas aguas de la literatura fantástica.

Sergio Guinot
www.artesecuencial.com

«Persino un bambino potrebbe farlo». Quante volte abbiamo ascoltato questa frase durante una conversazione informale su arte contemporanea? La stessa affermazione si potrebbe facilmente applicare alla creazione di personaggi fantastici e mitologici: a prima vista, non sembra così difficile disegnare una creatura simile a un orco, a un elfo, o a un drago. Tuttavia, come potrà testimoniare chiunque abbia cercato di disegnare una creatura fantastica partendo da zero, il compito è abbastanza più arduo di quanto sembrerebbe a prima vista. Infatti, non basta ritagliare e copiare «pezzi» delle grandi creature mitologiche classiche per ottenere un risultato con testa e piedi (è chiaro che si tratta di una metafora, infatti, le creature mitologiche non hanno bisogno né di testa né di piedi). Per non parlare della complessità derivante dalla creazione di un quadro mitologico che ospiti queste creature e gli attribuisca uno spazio con un equilibrio naturale perfettamente forgiato. Una sola incoerenza nell'impostazione potrebbe distruggere il mondo fantastico più ricco, complesso e studiato che possiamo immaginare.

A questa prima difficoltà se ne aggiunge una seconda: il genere fantastico porta con sé, incomprensibilmente, il marchio di «infantile» e «superficiale». Diciamo incomprensibilmente perché alla fin fine tutta la letteratura −dal denso, intrigante

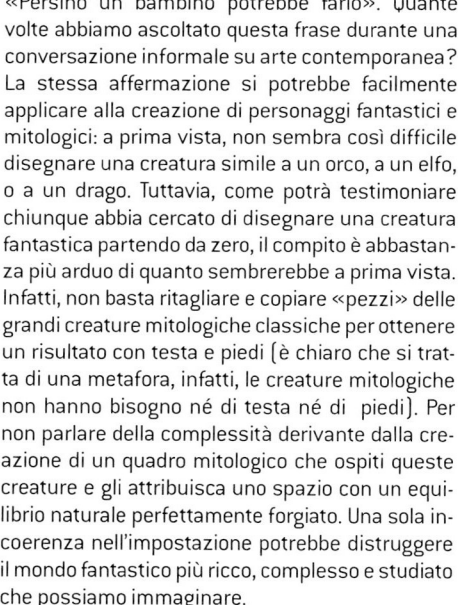

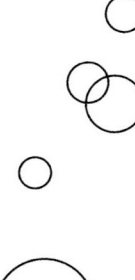

e barocco *Ulisse* di Joyce fino ai *bestsellers* come *Il Codice da Vinci*– è del genere fantastico. Neppure la cosiddetta novella realistica può essere considerata altro che fantasia con pretese di verosimiglianza. Tutto ciò rappresenta una difficoltà, perché affibbia al genere un peccato originale che solo può essere rimesso a base di trascendenze ed argomenti presumibilmente adulti.

Nonostante, il genere fantastico non è serio, ma neanche facile. Richiede uno spirito giocherellone e l'innocenza e la capacità di stupore che solo pochi adulti conservano una volta superata l'adolescenza.

Questo libro – un autentico catalogo morfologico destinato a professionisti del fumetto e dell'illustrazione, ma anche agli amanti del genere fantastico – riunisce più di 500 personaggi, la maggior parte dei quali sono disegnati partendo da zero. Concepito come una fonte di idee per il creativo, alcune di esse totalmente stravaganti ed altre abbastanza vicine alla verosimiglianza, questo volume è uno strumento di consultazione imprescindibile per chiunque voglia immergersi nelle burrascose acque della letteratura fantastica.

Sergio Guinot
www.artesecuencial.com

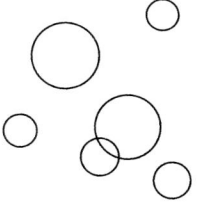

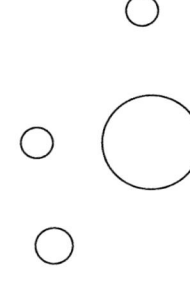

«Até uma criança o poderia fazer». Quantas vezes já ouvimos esta frase numa conversa informal sobre arte contemporânea? A mesma afirmação poderia aplicar-se facilmente à criação de personagens fantásticas e mitológicas: à primeira vista não parece muito difícil desenhar uma criatura semelhante a um orc, um elfo ou um dragão. Contudo, e como poderá confirmar qualquer pessoa que tenha tentando desenhar uma criatura fantástica a partir de zero, a tarefa é bastante mais complicada do que pode parecer num princípio. Ao efectuar esta tarefa não basta cortar e colar as «peças» das criaturas das grandes mitologias clássicas para obter um resultado com pés e cabeça (isto num sentido metafórico claro, porque num sentido literal as criaturas mitológicas não precisam de ter pés nem cabeça). E isso para não falar da dificuldade que representa a criação de um enquadramento mitológico que permita incluir essas criaturas e dar-lhes um espaço num equilíbrio natural perfeitamente conseguido. Uma só incoerência na planificação pode acabar com o mundo fantástico mais rico, complexo e estudado que possamos imaginar.

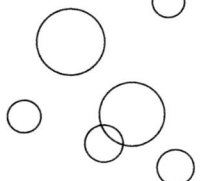

A esta primeira dificuldade soma-se uma segunda: o género fantástico carrega, de forma incompreensível, o estigma de «infantil» e «superficial». E dizemos de forma incompreensível porque afinal toda a literatura, desde o denso, complicado e barroco *Ulisses* de Joyce até aos *bestsellers* como *O Código da Vinci*, são literatu-

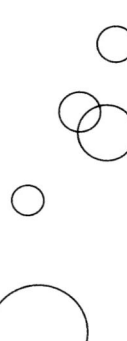

ra fantástica. Nem mesmo o chamado romance realista pode considerar-se mais do que fantasia com pretensões de veracidade. E isto acaba por ser uma dificuldade porque faz com que o género carregue um pecado original que só se pode redimir com uma transcendência e uns argumentos supostamente adultos.

Apesar de tudo, o género fantástico não é sério, embora também não seja fácil. Requer um espírito brincalhão e a inocência e capacidade de admiração que apenas um pequeno número de adultos conservam depois de ultrapassar a adolescência.

Este livro —um verdadeiro catálogo morfológico que se destina aos profissionais da banda desenhada e da ilustração, mas também aos amantes do género fantástico— reúne mais de 500 personagens criadas, na sua grande maioria, a partir do zero. Concebido como uma fonte de ideias para os criadores, algumas delas completamente disparatadas e outras bastante próximas da veracidade, este volume é um instrumento de consulta imprescindível para aqueles que pretendem mergulhar nas águas tempestuosas da literatura fantástica.

Sergio Guinot
www.artesecuencial.com

Beasts
Bestias
Bestie
Monstros

Beasts are bizarre creatures, half man and half animal. Although their origin is lost in the mists of time, legends speak of unnatural unions, curses from powerful witchcraft or the whim of a capricious god. Looked down upon by mortals, beasts are solitary and tranquil beings that prefer to lurk in the background. However, if they feel threatened, they emerge from hiding to fight alongside their allies, and are practically an unconquerable force.

Las bestias son criaturas extrañas, mitad hombre y mitad animal. Aunque su origen se pierde en las brumas del tiempo, las leyendas hablan de uniones antinaturales, maldiciones de poderosas hechiceras o del antojo de algún dios caprichoso. Despreciadas por los mortales, las bestias son seres solitarios y tranquilos que prefieren mantenerse ocultos. A pesar de ello, si sienten su vida amenazada, emergen al mundo exterior para combatir junto a sus aliados, conformando una fuerza de choque prácticamente invencible.

Le bestie sono creature strane, metà uomo e metà animale. Anche se la loro origine si perde nella notte dei tempi, le leggende parlano di unioni contro natura, maledizioni di potenti streghe o delle voglie di qualche dio capriccioso. Disprezzate dai mortali, le bestie sono esseri solitari e tranquilli che preferiscono restare nascosti. Nonostante ciò, sentono che la loro vita è a rischio; emergono dal mondo esterno per combattere insieme ai loro alleati, dando vita a forze praticamente invincibili.

Os monstros são criaturas estranhas, metade homem metade animal. Embora a sua origem se perca nas brumas do tempo, as lendas falam de uniões anti-naturais, maldições de poderosas feiticeiras ou o capricho de algum deus mimado. Desprezados pelos mortais, os monstros são seres solitários e tranquilos que preferem manter-se ocultos. Contudo quando sentem a sua vida ameaçada, surgem no mundo exterior para combater ao lado dos seus aliados, formando uma força de intervenção praticamente invencível.

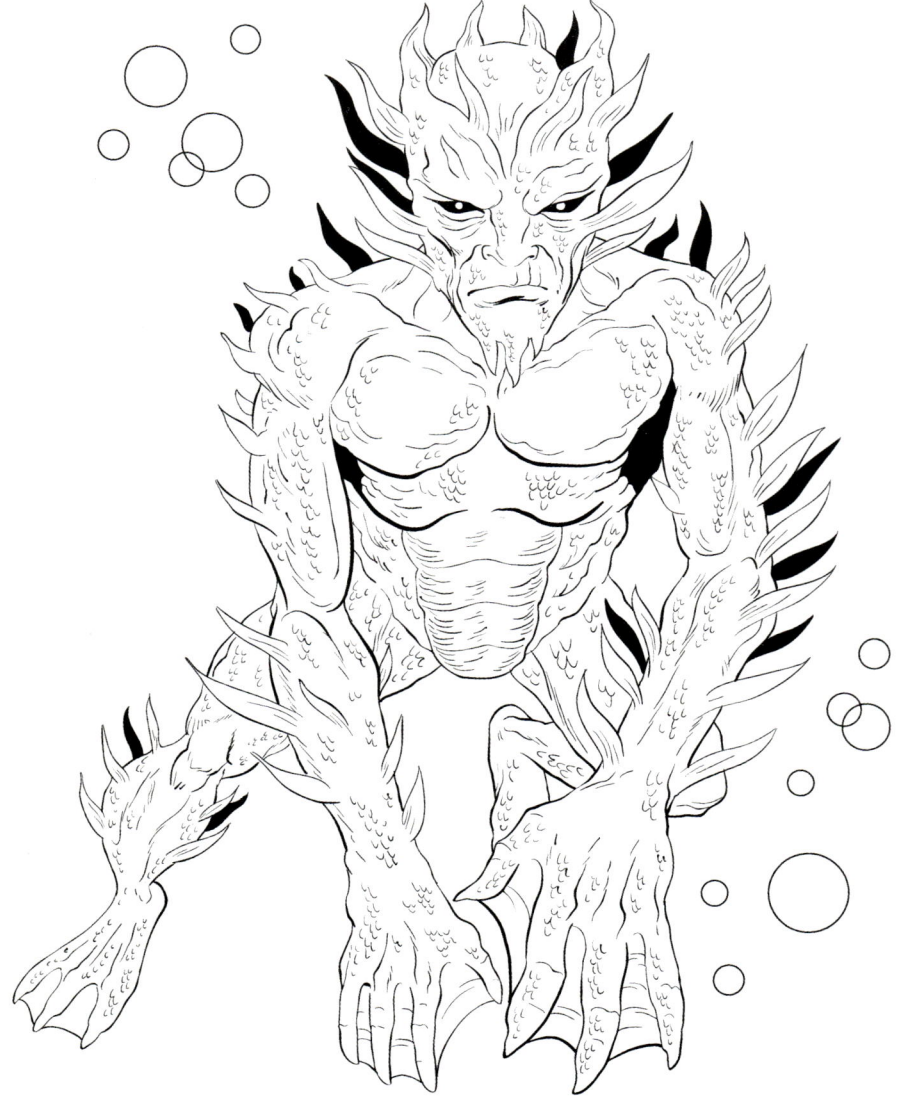

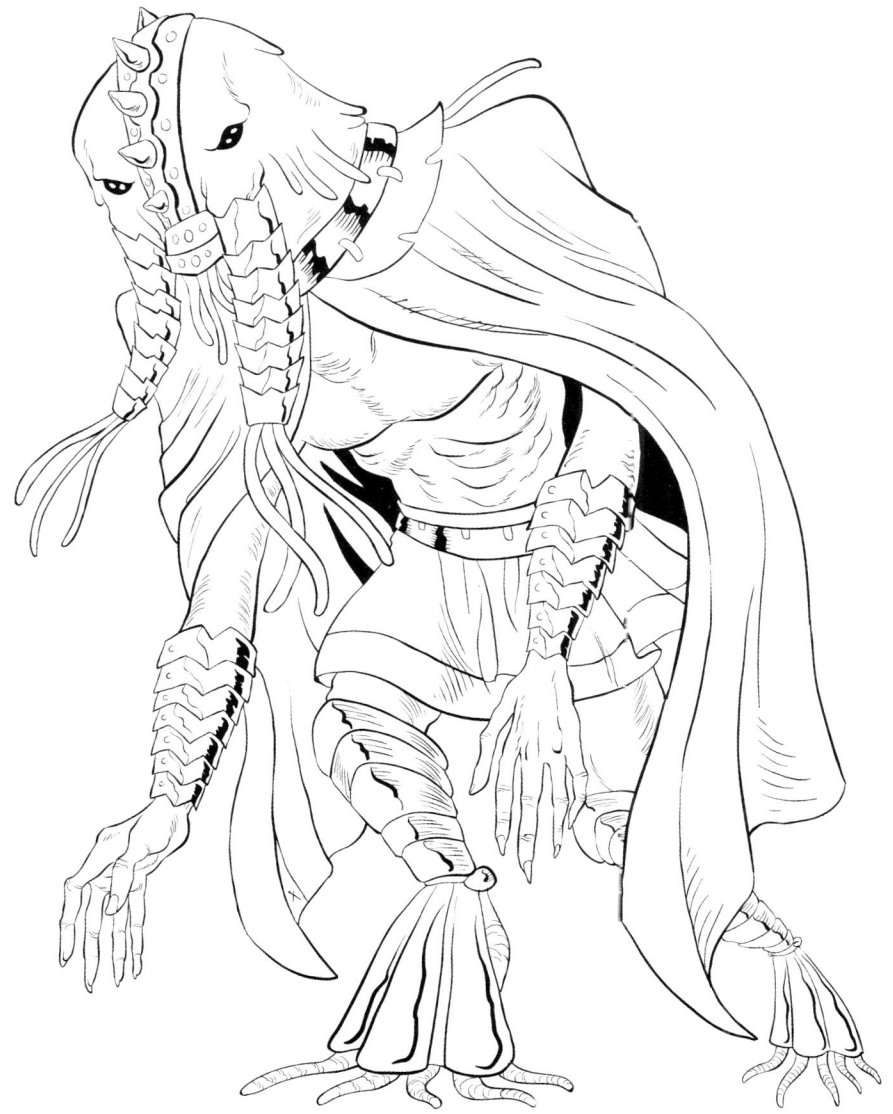

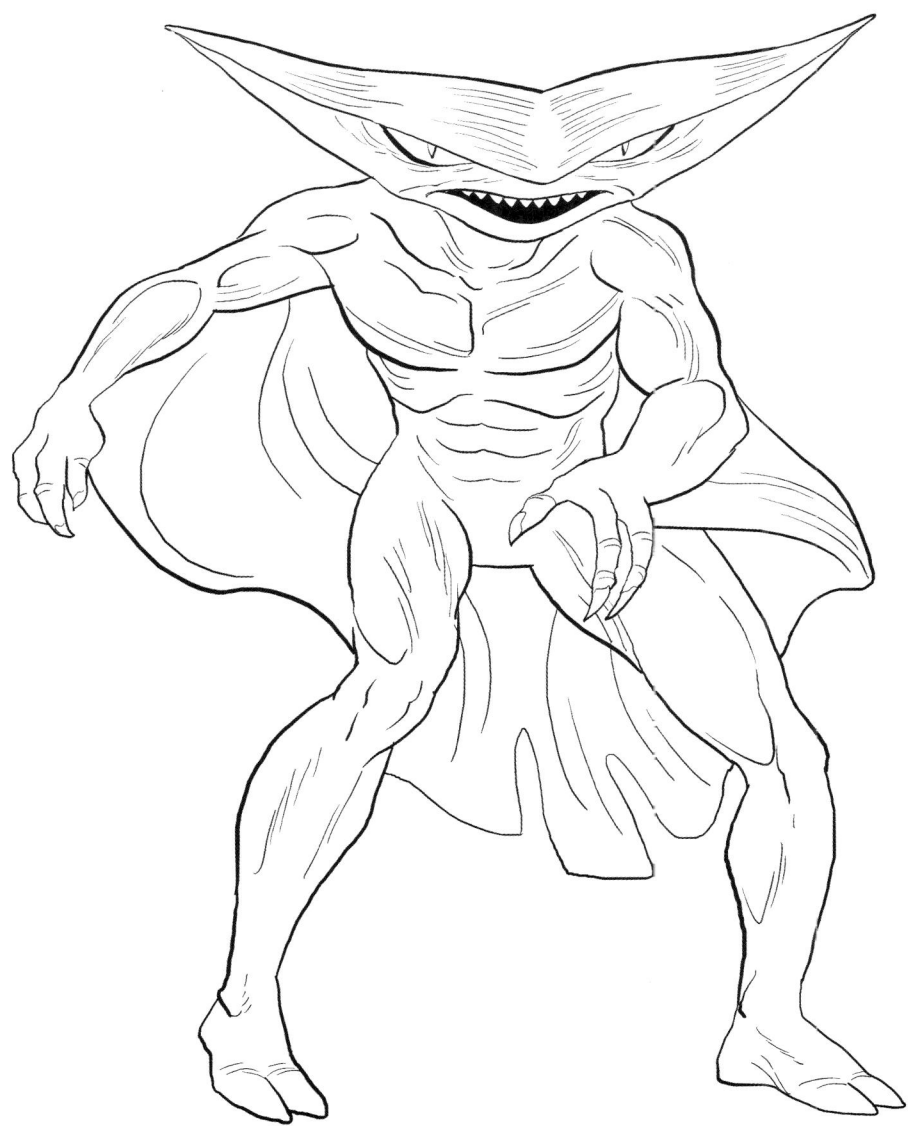

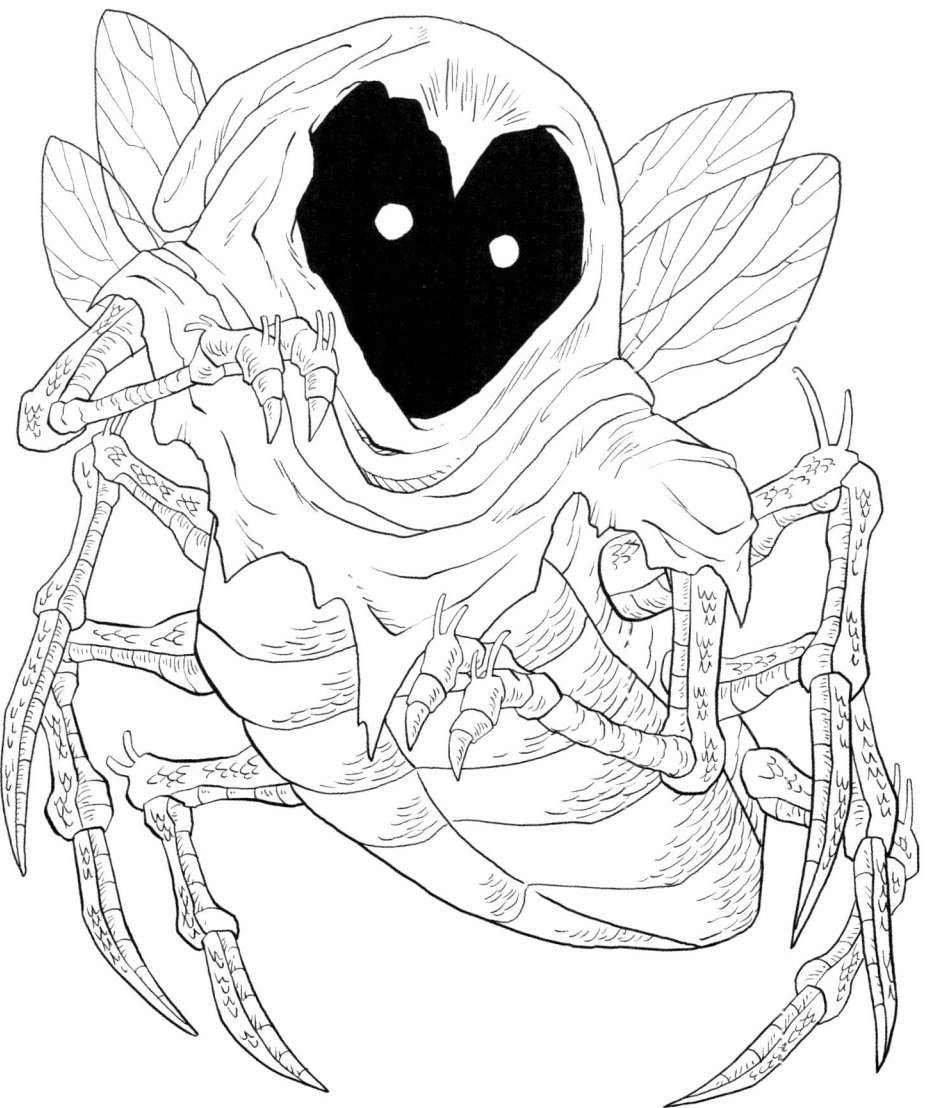

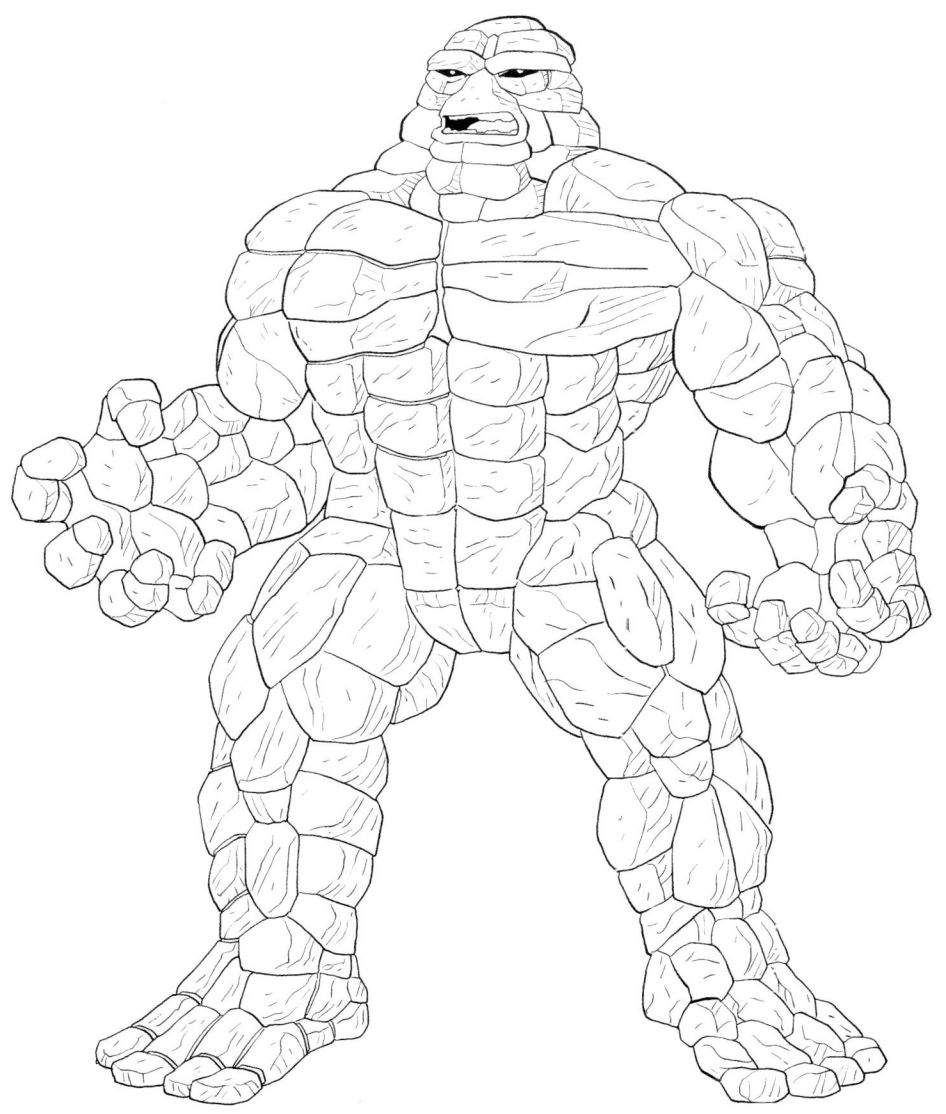

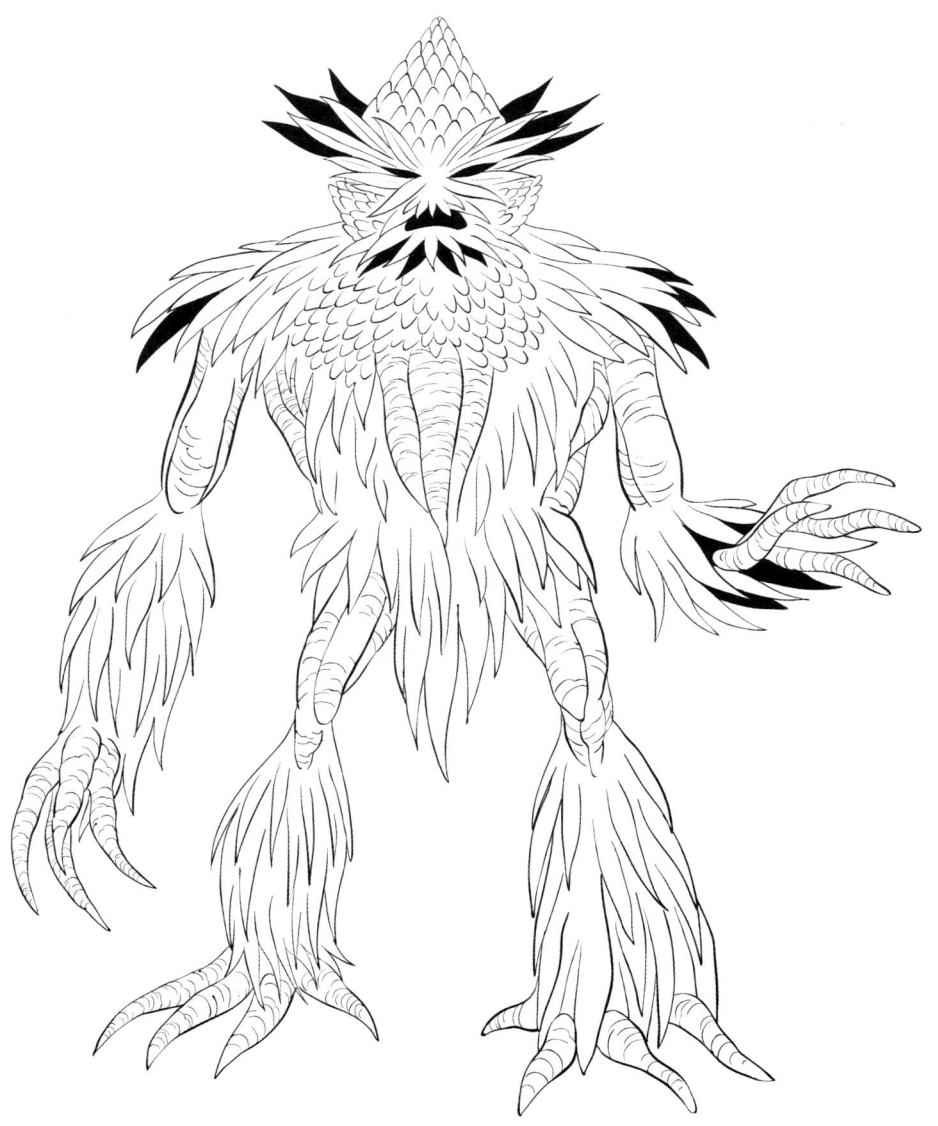

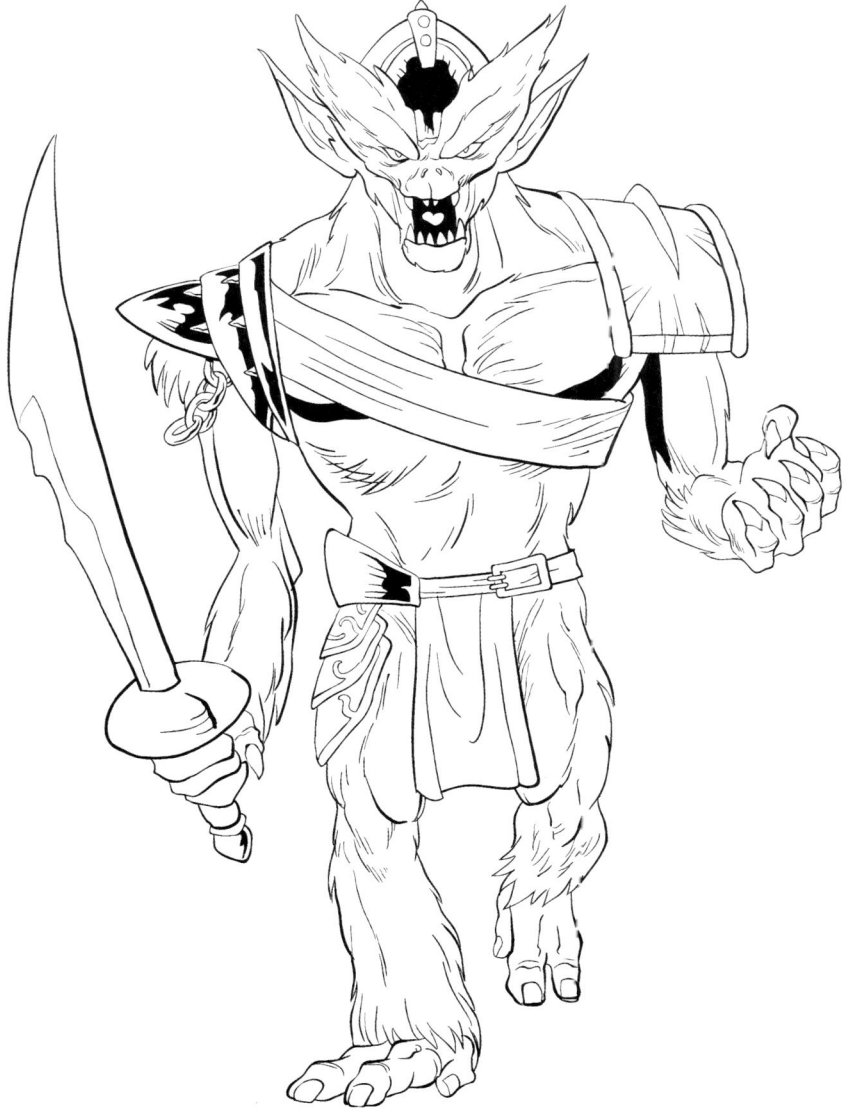

Mortals
Mortales
Mortali
Mortais

In a world where the law of the most powerful and the tyranny of steel prevail, many races of mortal beings fight for survival. From the longevous elves, who can live more than 500 years, to the tiny tersinios, whose brief existence last no longer than a decade, they all live life to the full as a non-stop adventure. Perhaps it is for this reason that mortals possess a mighty inner strength and determination capable of changing the face of the world and even the destiny of the gods.

En un mundo en el que impera la ley del más fuerte y la tiranía del acero, existen varias razas de seres mortales que luchan por sobrevivir. Desde los longevos elfos, que pueden llegar a vivir más de 500 años, hasta los diminutos tersinios, cuya fugaz existencia se apaga antes de una década, todos exprimen la vida como una aventura constante. Quizá por ello los mortales poseen una gran fuerza interior y una determinación capaz de cambiar la faz del mundo e incluso el destino de los dioses.

In un mondo in cui dominano la legge del più forte e la tirannia, esistono varie razze di esseri mortali che lottano per la sopravvivenza. Dai longevi elfi che possono vivere oltre 500 anni fino ai piccoli tersinios la cui fugace esistenza non supera i dieci anni, tutti esprimono la vita come una costante avventura. Forse è proprio per questo che i mortali possiedono una grande forza interiore e una determinazione che li rende capaci di cambiare il mondo e persino il destino degli dei.

Num mundo onde impera a lei do mais forte e a tirania do aço, existem várias raças de seres mortais que lutam para sobreviver. Desde os longevos elfos, que podem viver até mais de 500 anos, até aos diminutos tersinios, cuja fugaz existência se extingue antes de uma década, todos encaram a vida como uma aventura constante. Talvez por isso os mortais possuem uma grande força interior e uma determinação capazes de mudar a face do mundo e mesmo o destino dos deuses.

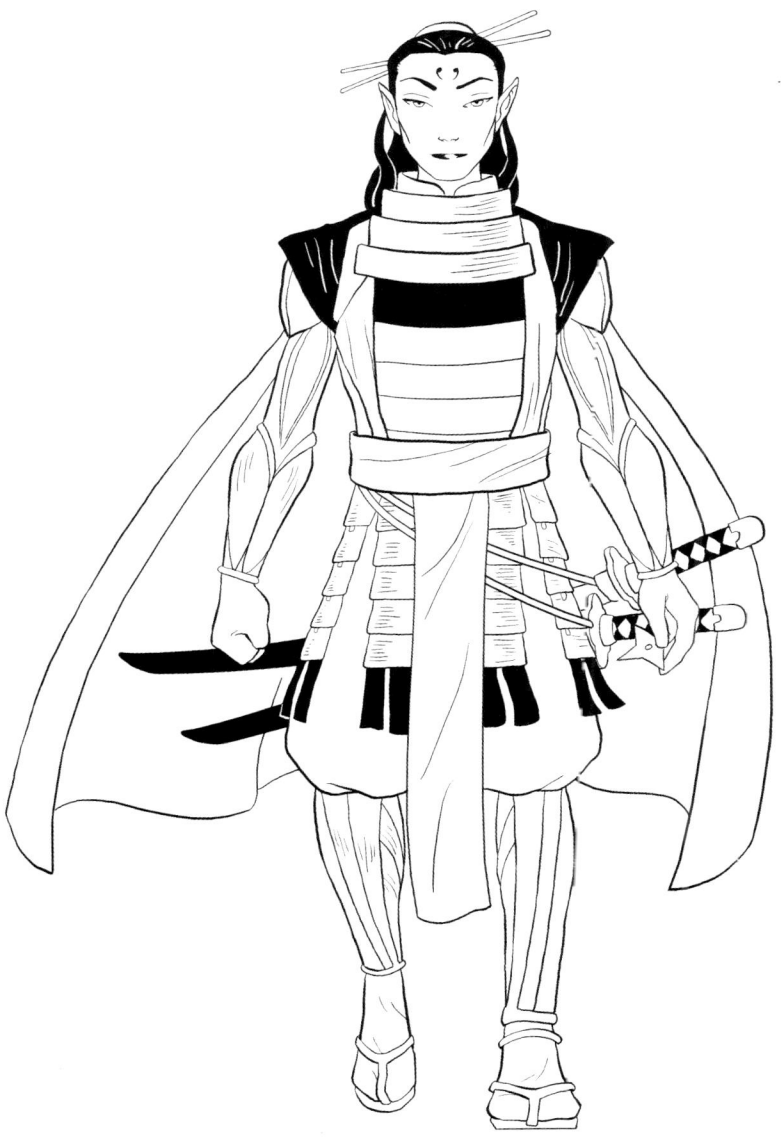

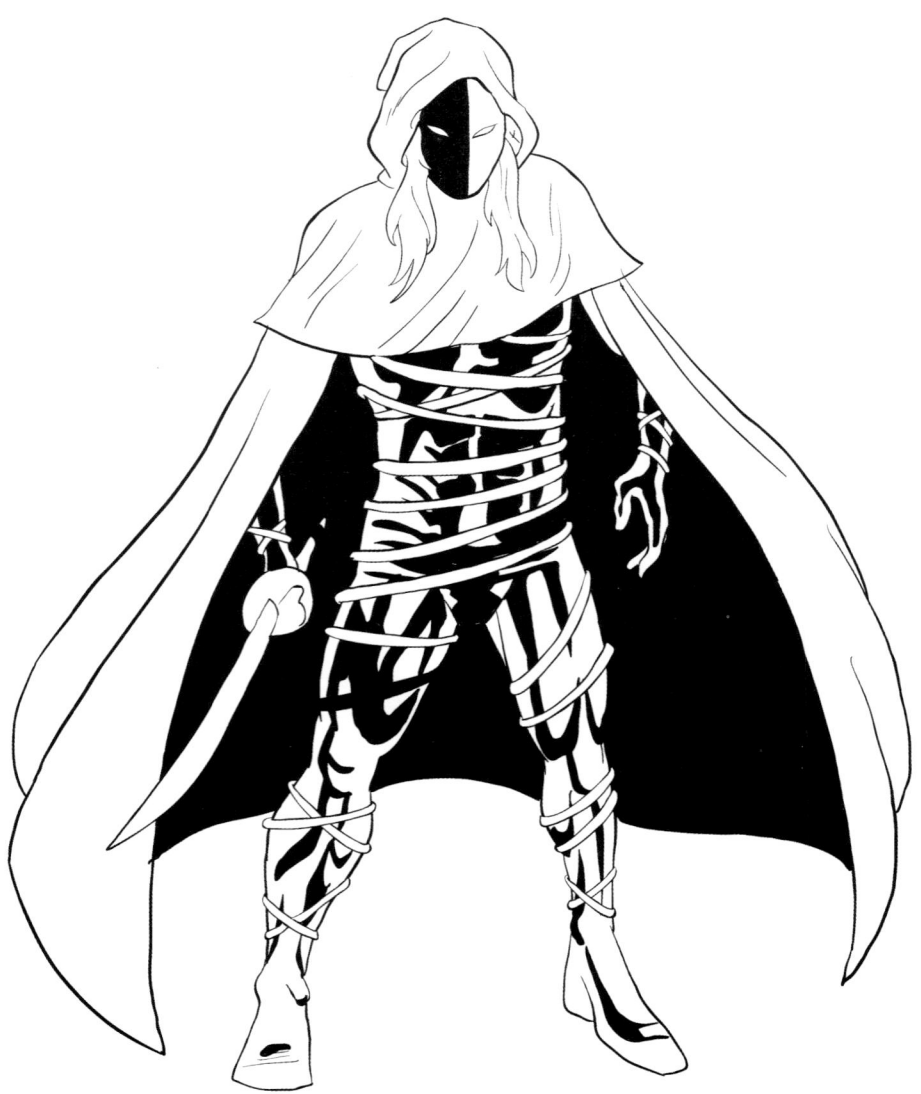

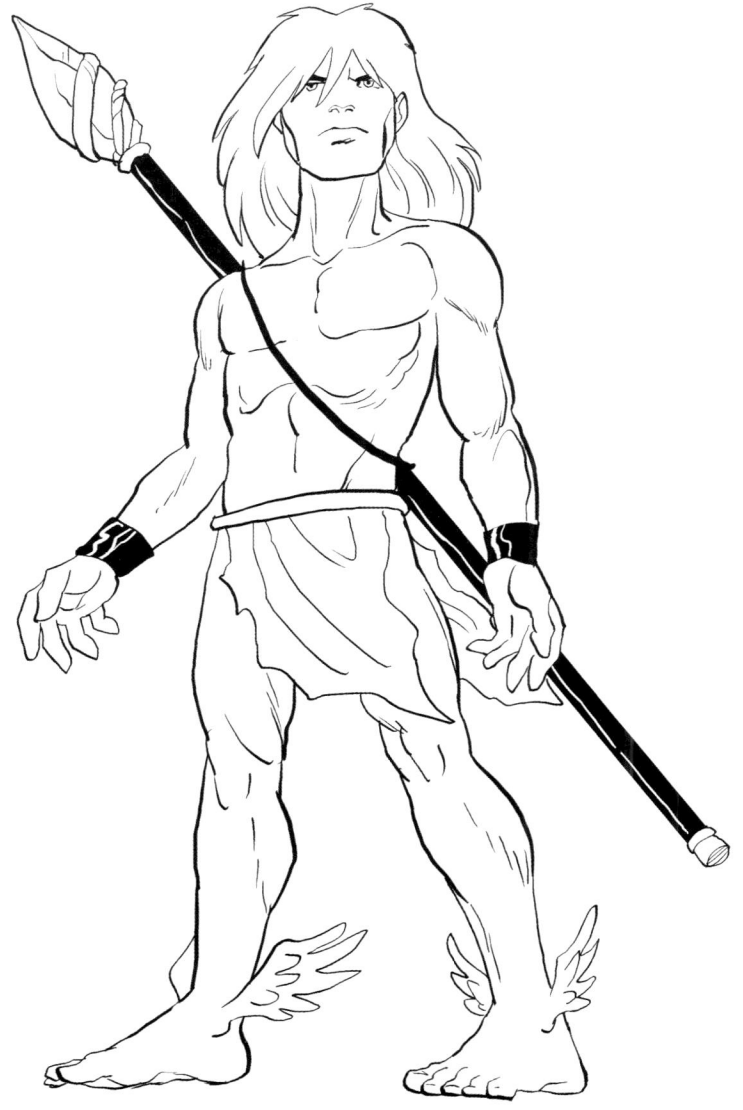

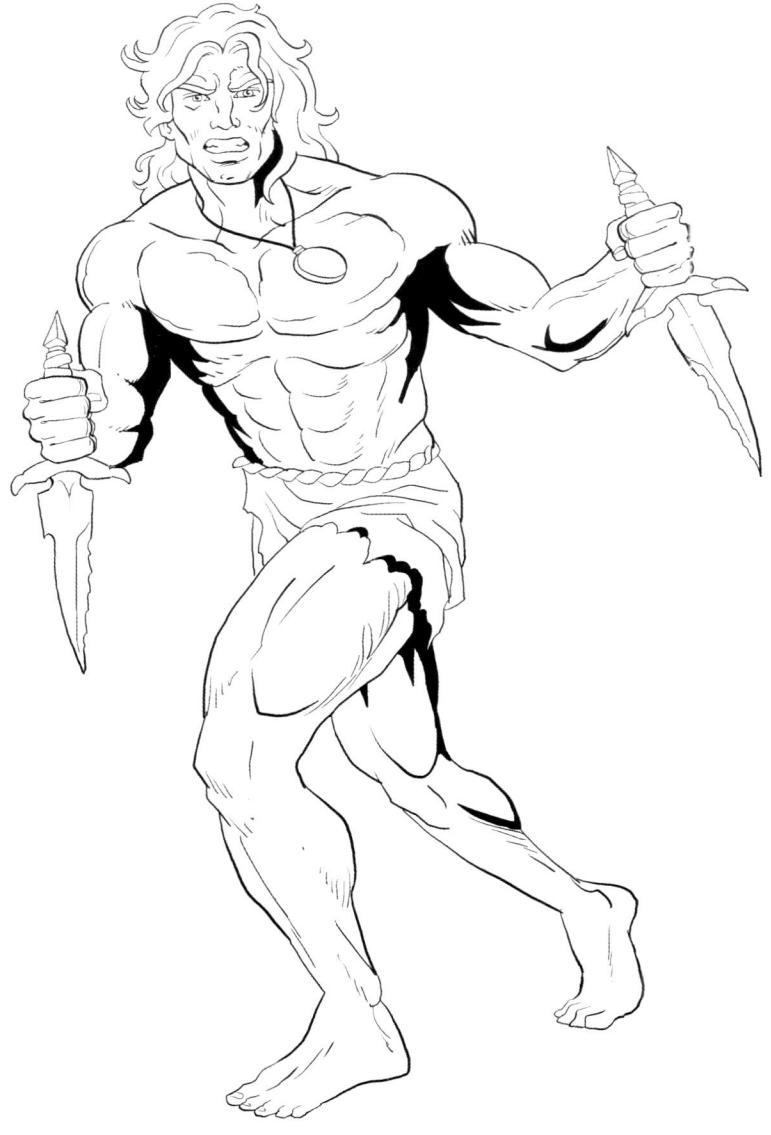

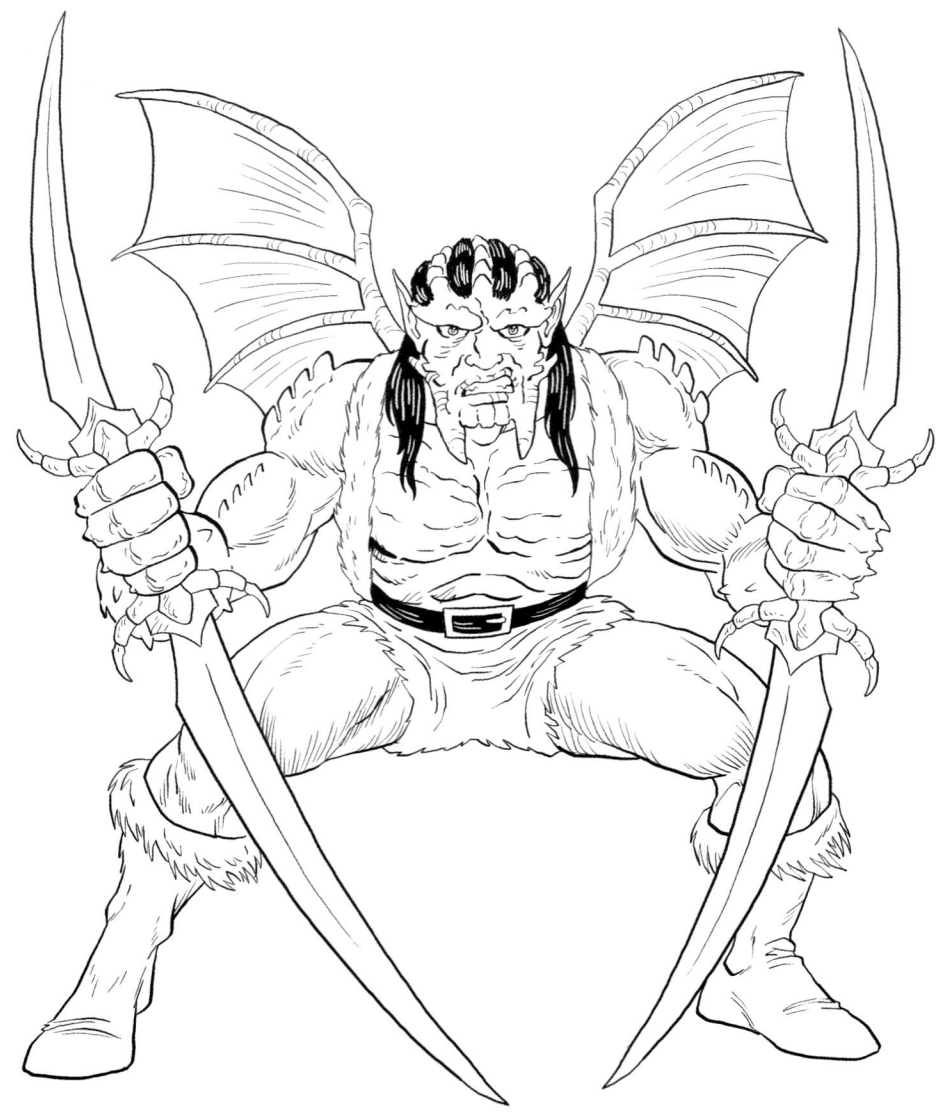

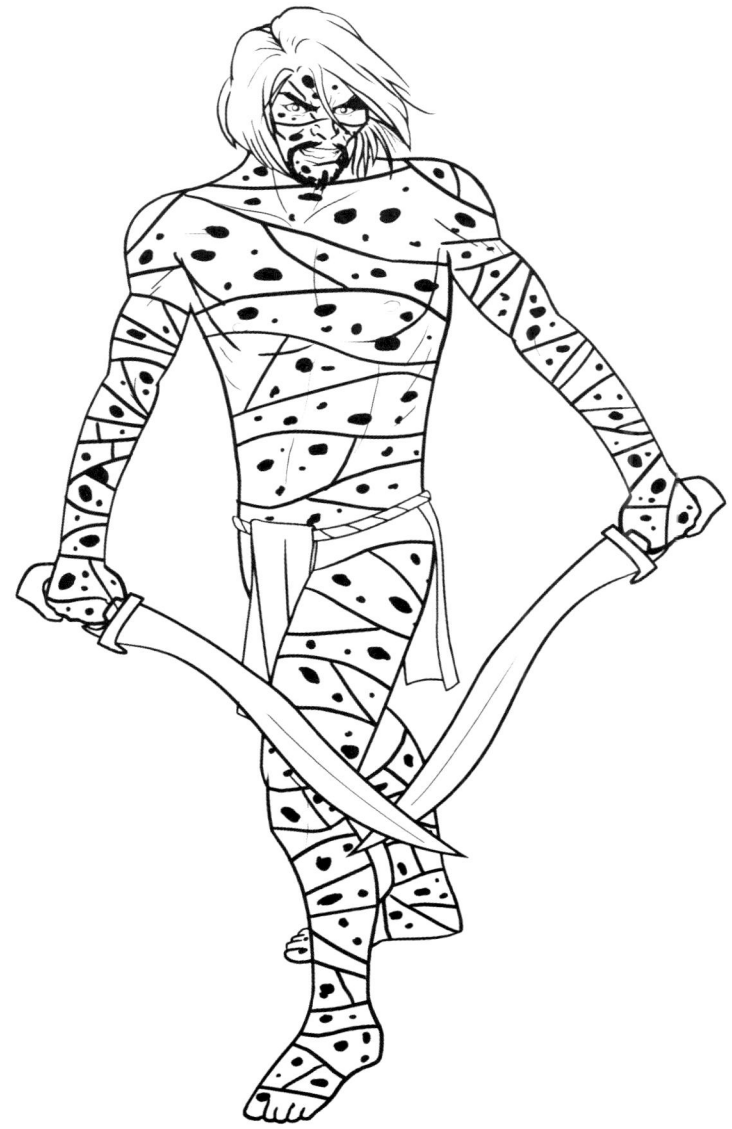

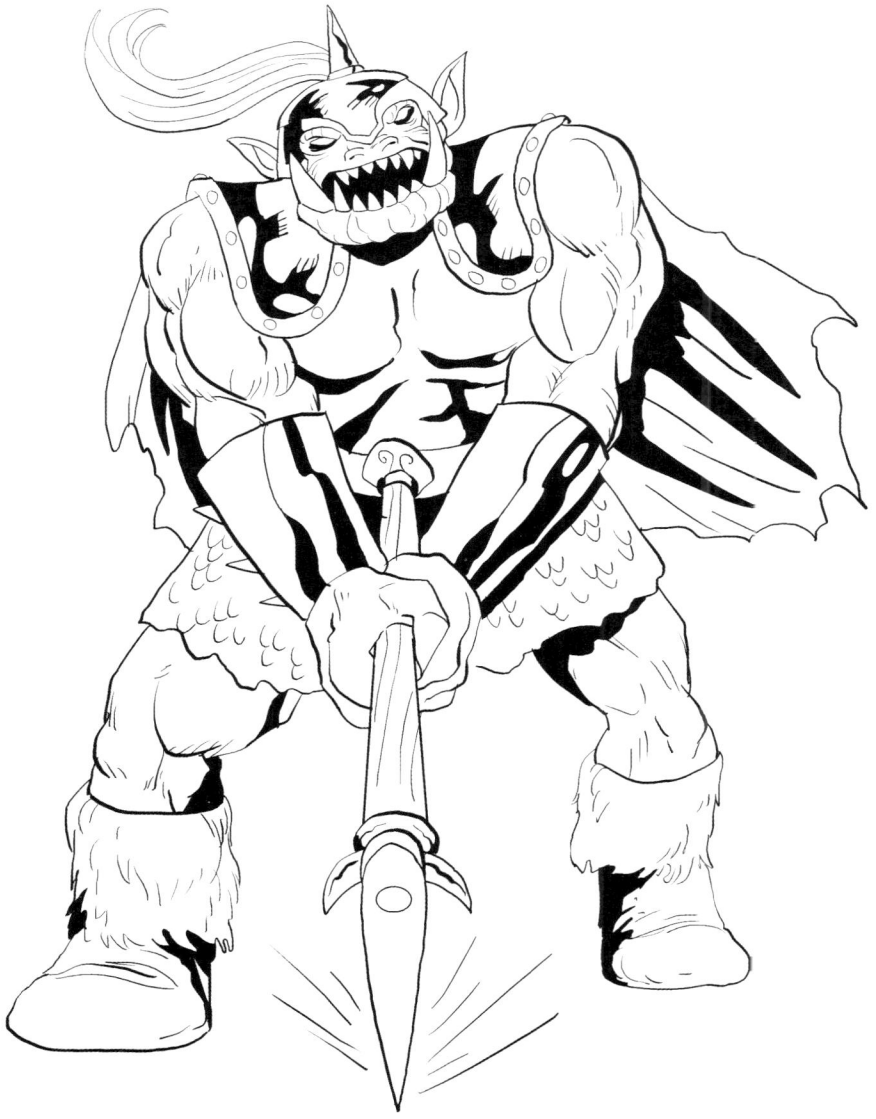

Gods and half-gods
Dioses y semidioses
Dei e semidei
Deuses e semideuses

Only by the mere mention of the omnipotent beings that are the gods, mortals, beasts, wizards and demons pale into insignificance. Worshipped, feared and idolized, between them they fight colossal battles with universal powers that go beyond the realms of our understanding. The half-gods, the result of the carnal union between a god and a mortal are superior and admired beings likened to heroes who roam the world performing heroic deeds that one day will become legends.

Los dioses son entidades omnipotentes cuya sola mención empequeñece a mortales, bestias, magos y demonios. Venerados, temidos e idolatrados, libran entre sí titánicas batallas utilizando fuerzas universales que van más allá de toda comprensión. Por su parte, los semidioses, fruto de la unión carnal entre un dios y un mortal, son seres superiores y admirados como héroes destinados a vagar por el mundo realizando proezas increíbles que se convierten en leyendas.

Gli dei sono essere onnipotenti la cui sola menzione rende insignificanti mortali, bestie, maghi e demoni. Venerati, temuti e idolatrati, si scontrano in titaniche battaglie utilizzando forze universali che vanno oltre ogni capacità di comprensione. Da parte loro, i semidei, frutto dell'unione carnale tra dei e mortali, sono esseri superiori, ammirati come eroi, destinati a vagare per il mondo per compiere atti prodigiosi e incredibili che finiscono per diventare ben presto leggende.

Os deuses são entidades omnipotentes que basta mencionar para os mortais, os monstros, os feiticeiros e os demónios se sentirem pequenos. Venerados, temidos e idolatrados, travam entre si batalhas titânicas utilizando forças universais que estão para lá de qualquer compreensão. Por outro lado os semideuses, fruto da união carnal entre um deus e um mortal, são seres superiores e admirados como heróis, destinados a viajar pelo mundo e a efectuar proezas incríveis que rapidamente se transformam em lendas.

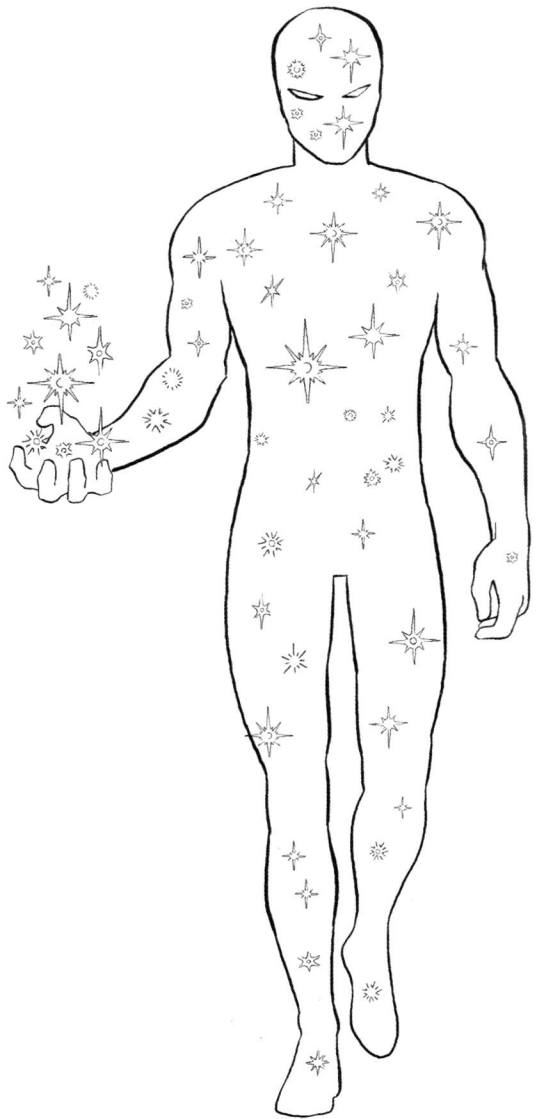

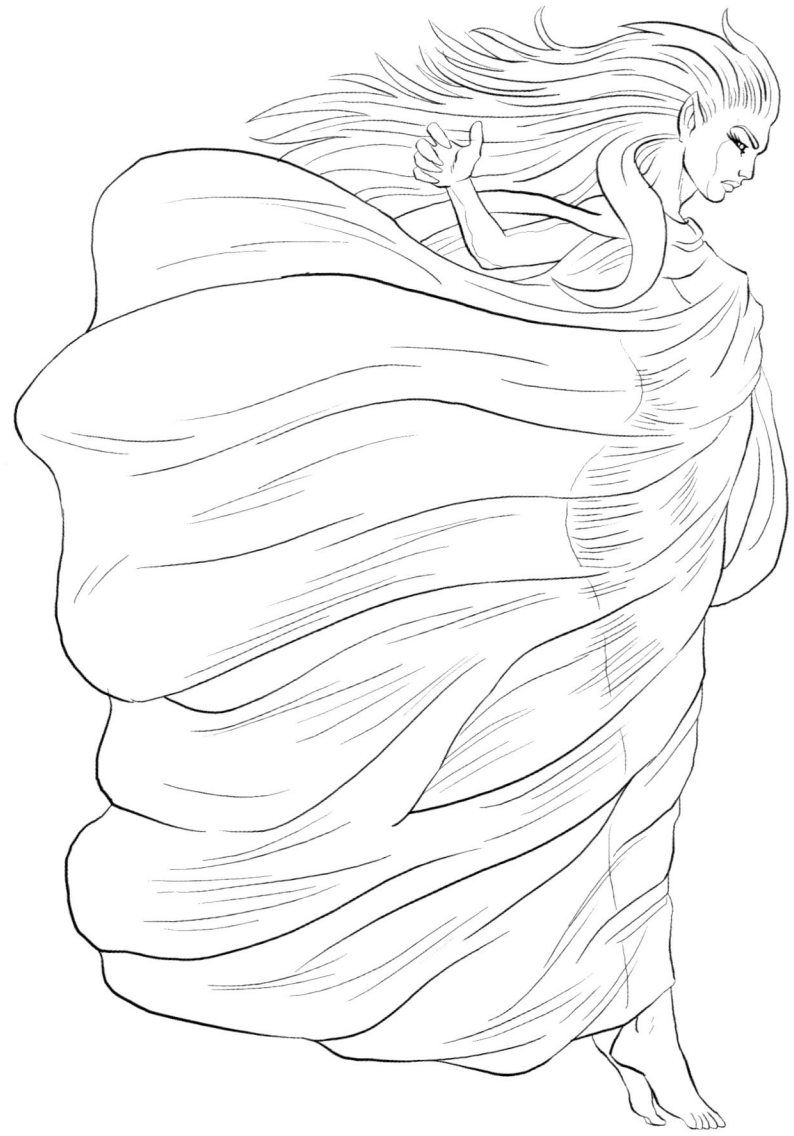

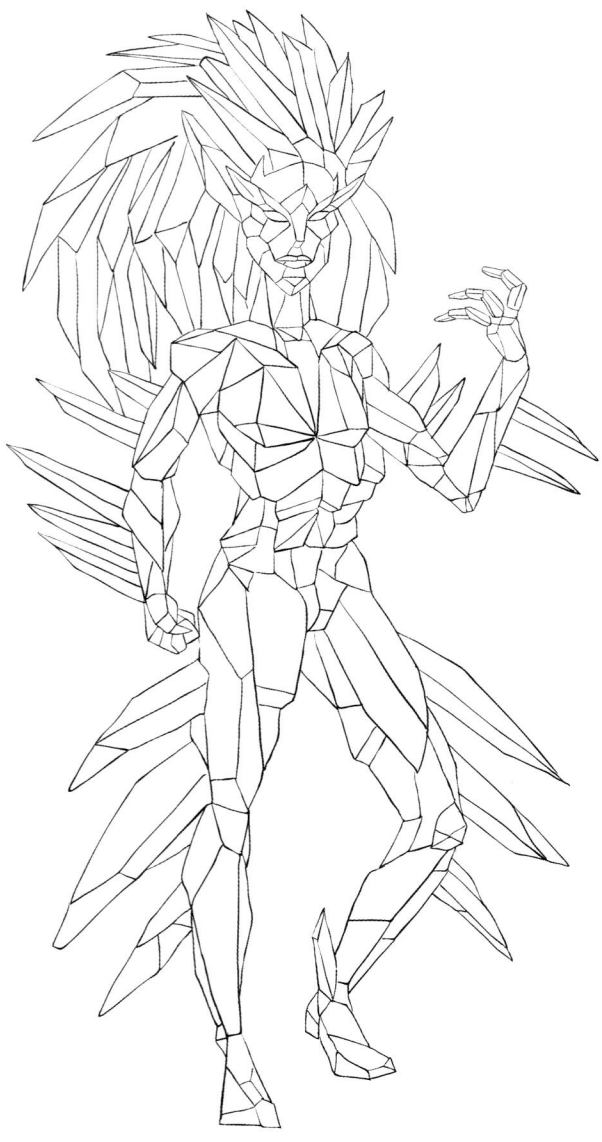

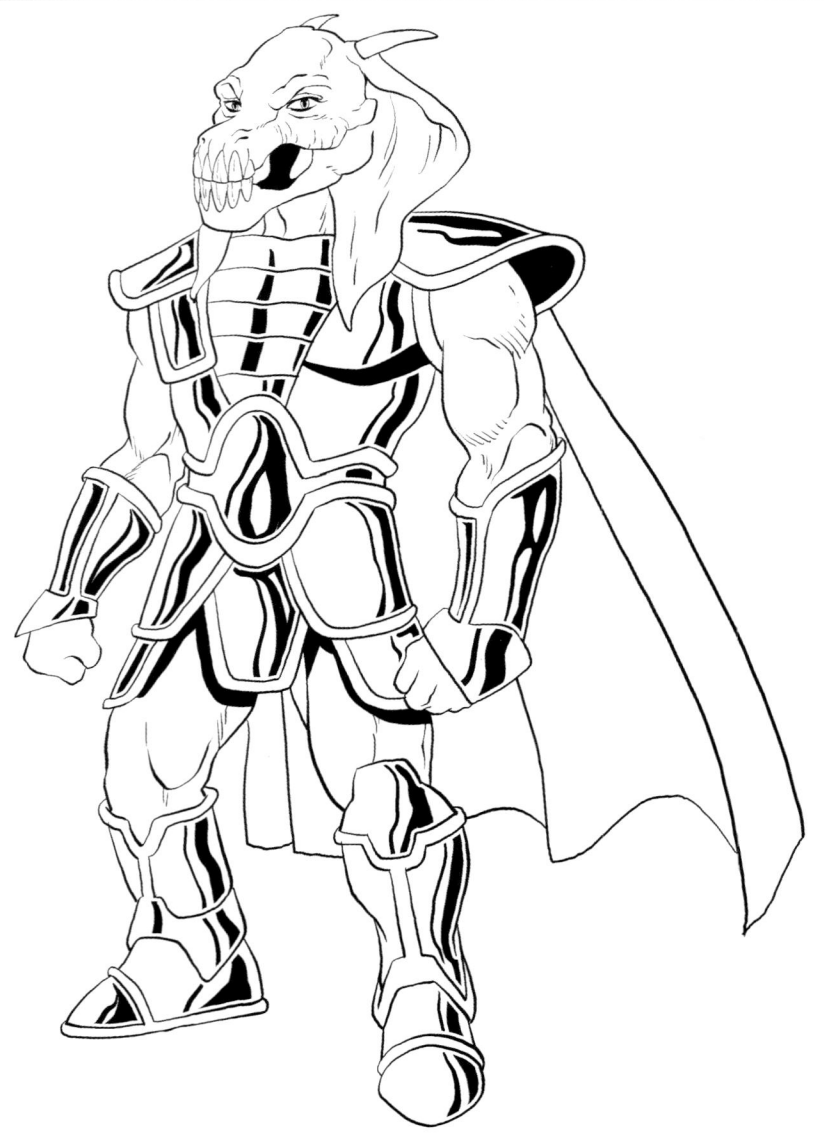

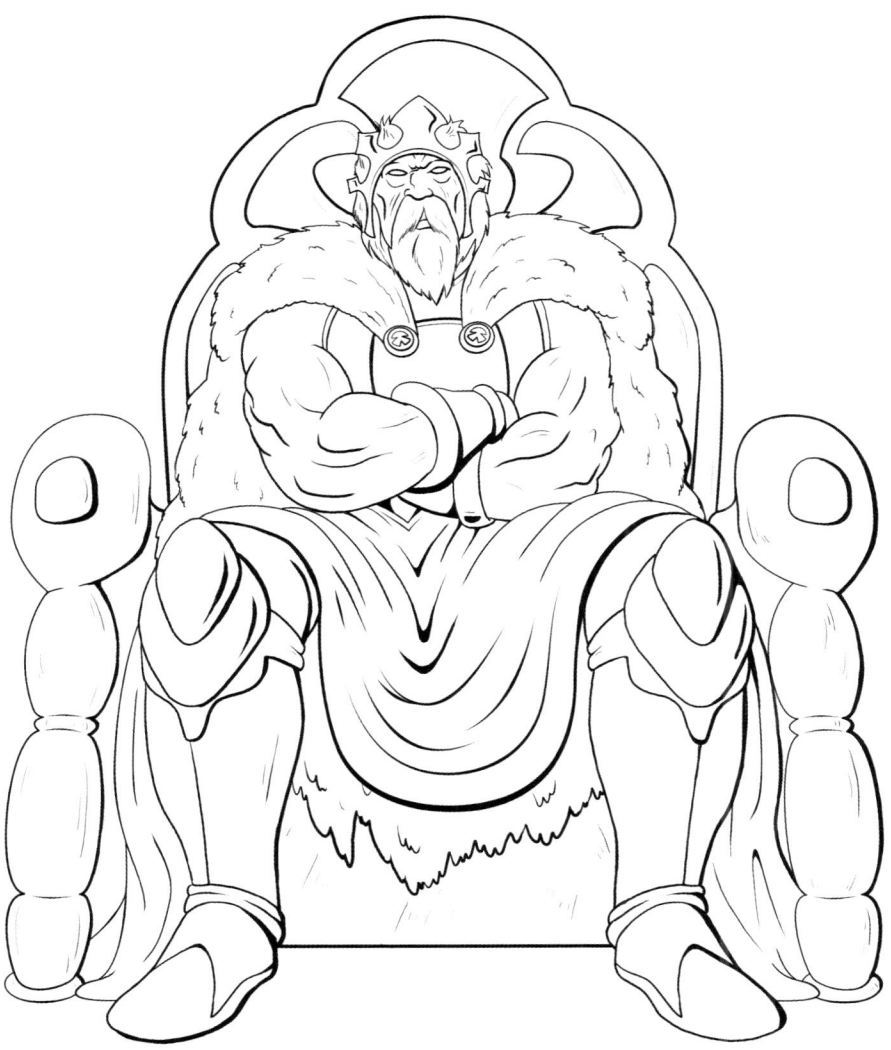

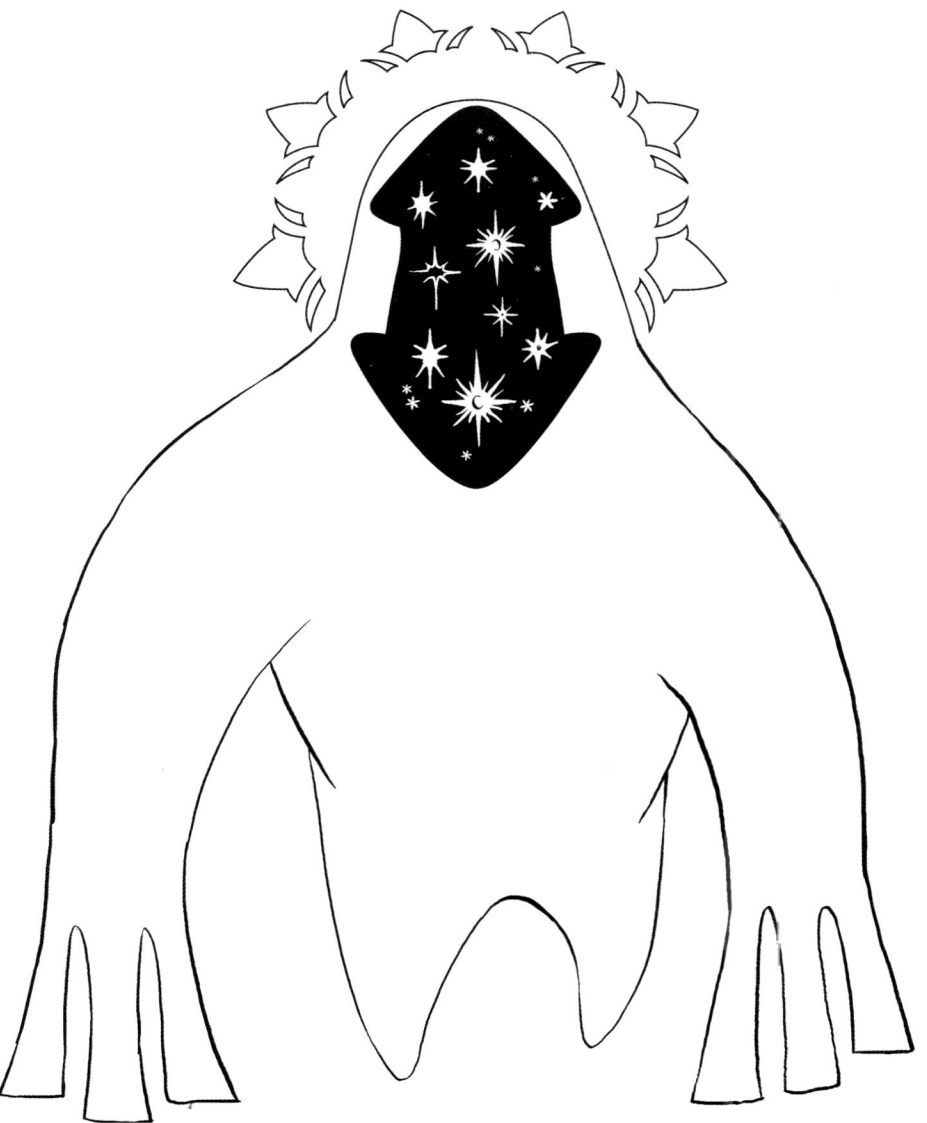

Animals
Animales
Animali
Animais

Animals wander the planet in a myriad of different shapes, colors and sizes. From the impressive swarms of millions of Duluds to the curious Sleg, the wild fauna coexists with man interpreting the role of the prey or hunter in an endless duel for survival. Animals have less developed brains and are normally used by other beings to carry out the hardest tasks, although some have become legends through the faithfulness that they profess for their masters.

Los animales se extienden por todo el planeta en una miríada de formas, colores y tamaños. Desde las impresionantes manadas de millones de Duluds hasta el insólito Sleg, la fauna salvaje convive con el hombre interpretando el papel de presa o el de cazador en un interminable duelo por la supervivencia. Los animales carecen de un cerebro desarrollado y suelen ser utilizados por otros seres para las tareas más duras, aunque algunos de ellos se han convertido en leyenda gracias a la fidelidad que profesaban por sus amos.

Gli animali sono presenti in tutto il pianeta sotto moltissime forme, colori e dimensioni diversi. Dagli incredibili stormi di milioni di Duluds fino all'insolito Sleg, la fauna selvatica convive con l'uomo interpretando il ruolo di preda o di cacciatore in un'interminabile lotta per la sopravvivenza. Gli animali non hanno un cervello sviluppato e solitamente sono utilizzati da altri esseri per svolgere le mansioni più pesanti, anche se alcuni di loro si sono convertiti in leggenda grazie alla fedeltà dimostrata nei confronti dei loro padroni.

Os animais encontram-se em todo o planeta sob uma miríade de formas, cores e tamanhos. Desde as impressionantes manadas de milhões de Duluds até ao insólito Sleg, a fauna selvagem convive com o homem, interpretando o papel de presa ou o de caçador num interminável duelo pela sobrevivência. Os animais não possuem um cérebro desenvolvido e costumam ser utilizados por outros seres para as tarefas mais duras, embora alguns deles se tenham transformado em lendas pelo carácter fiel demonstrado perante os seus donos.

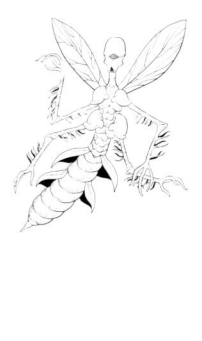

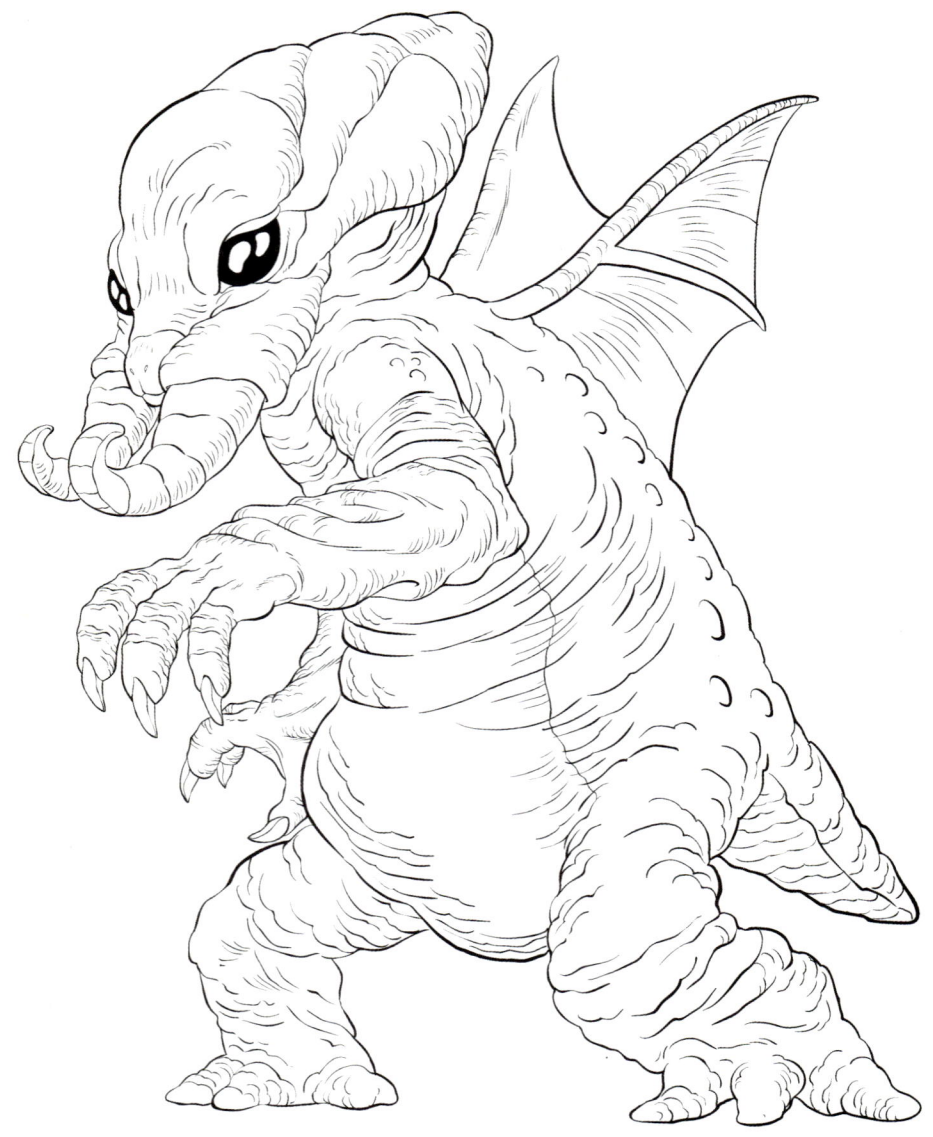

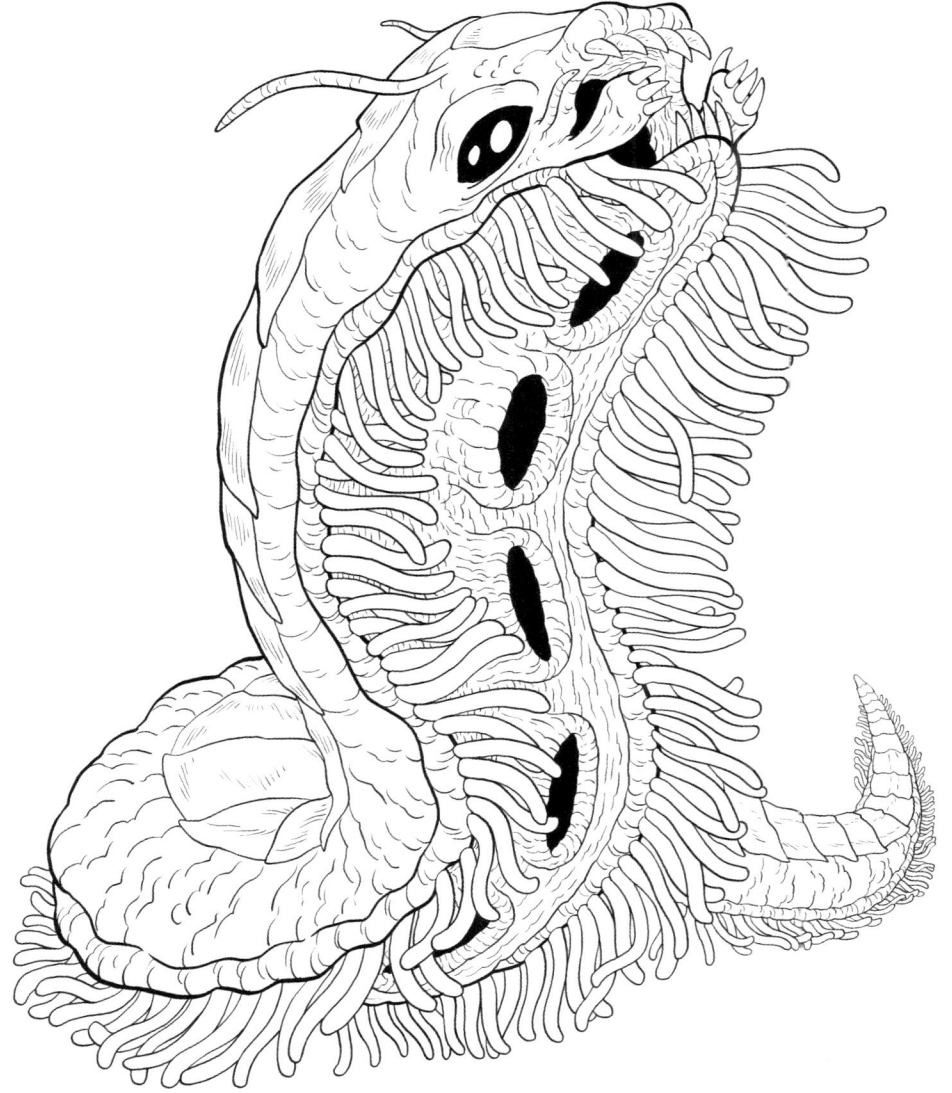

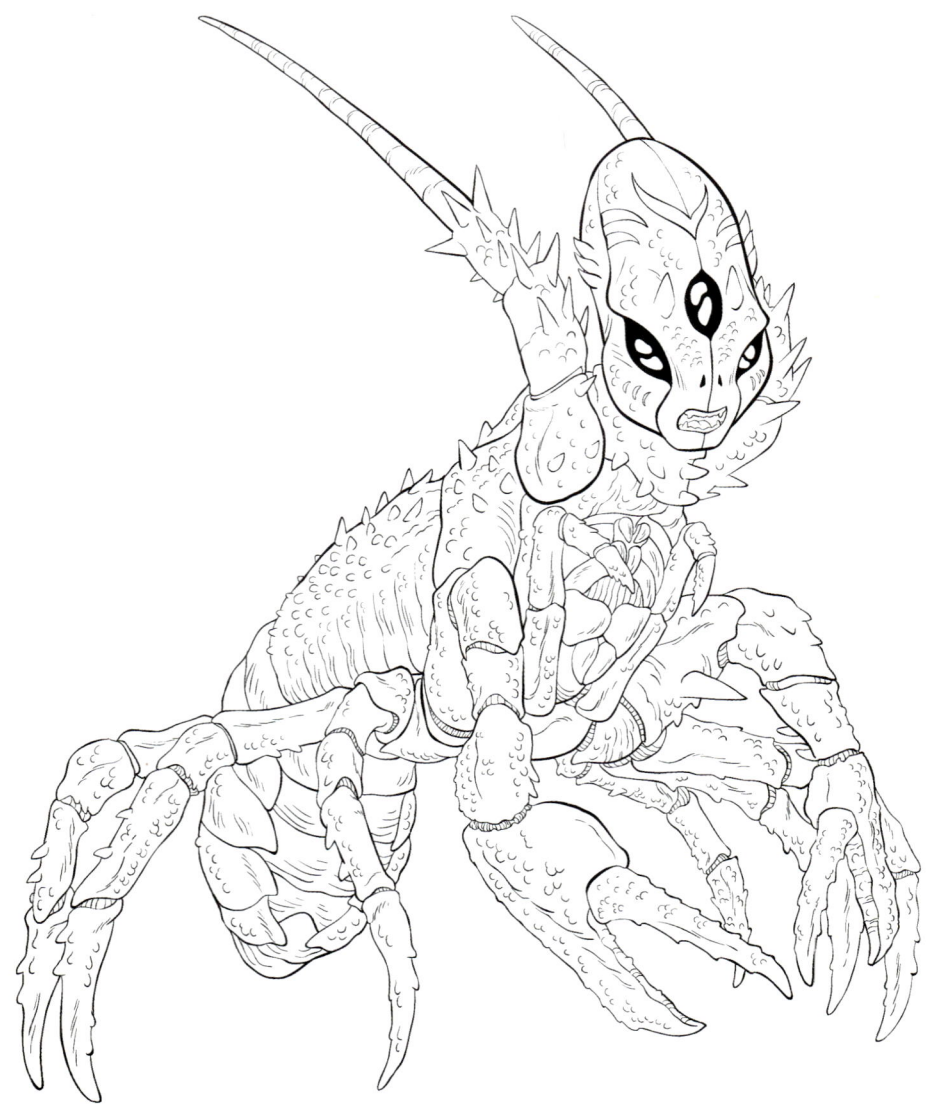

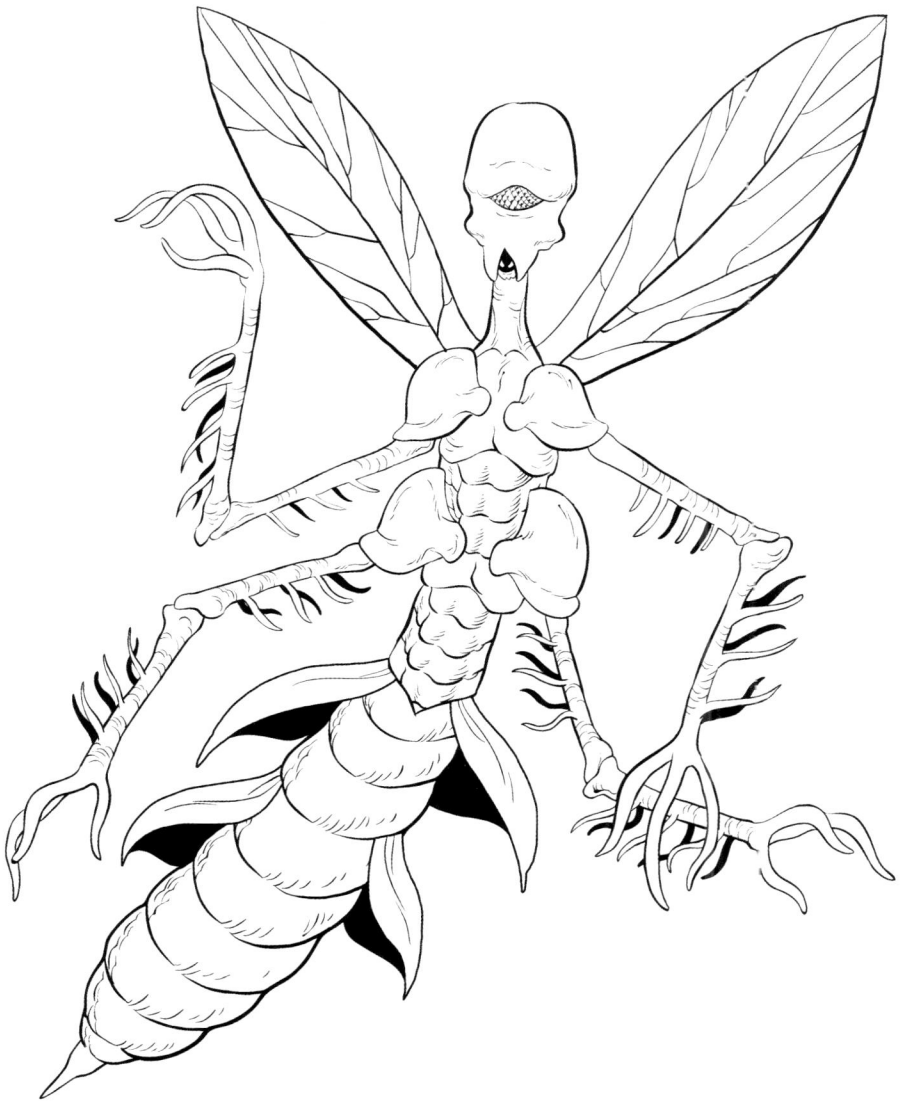

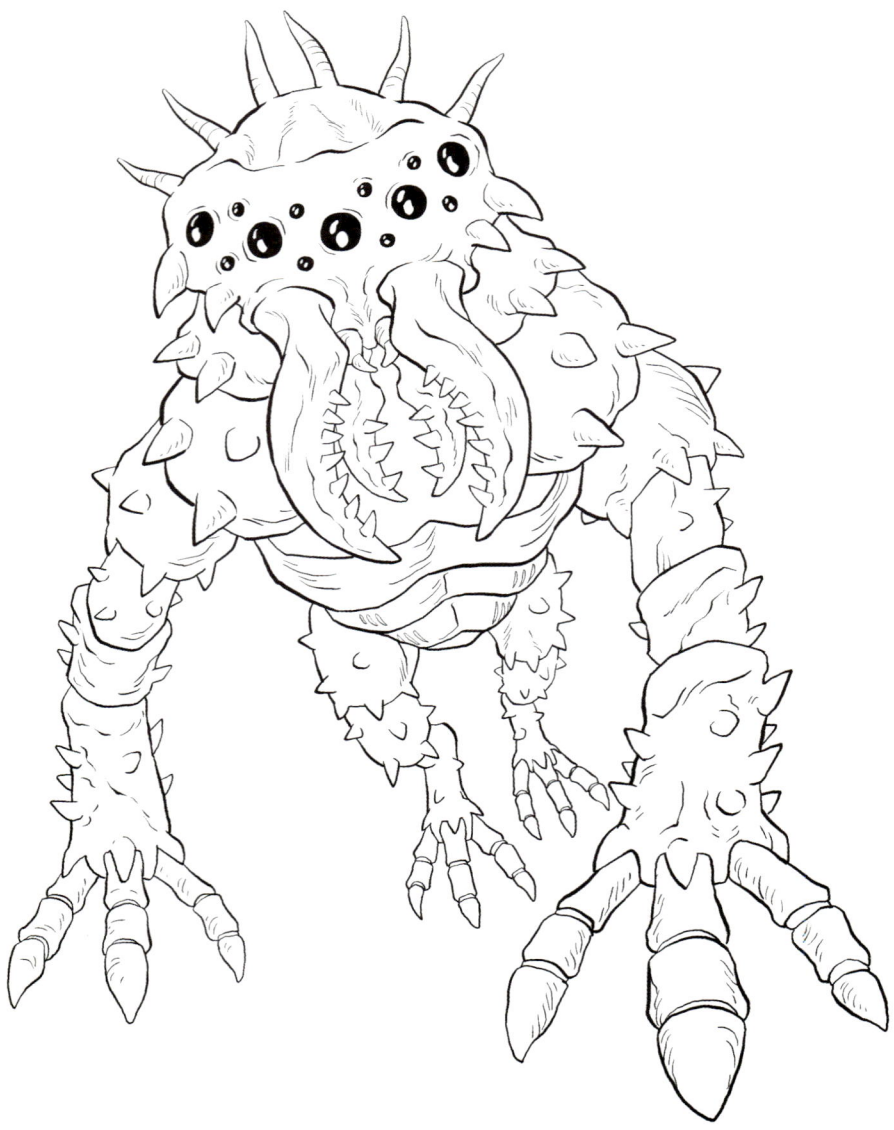

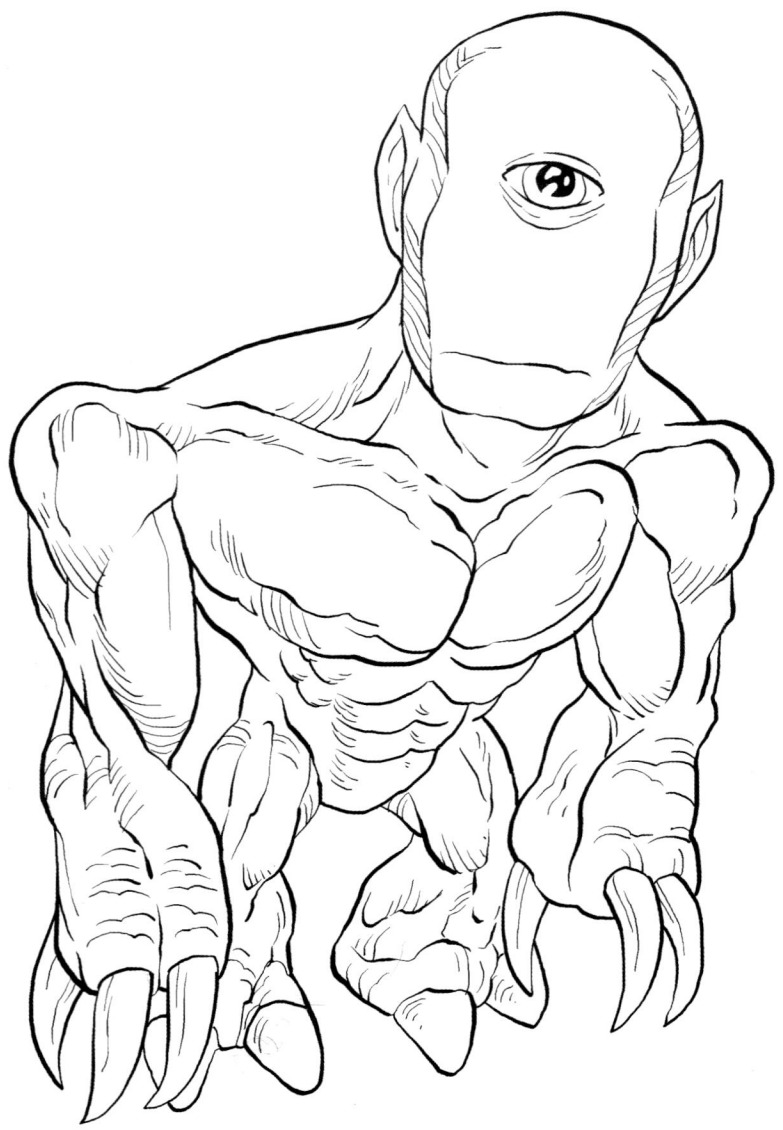

Demons
Demonios
Demoni
Demónios

The servants of Evil are malformed odious creatu res with a sole horrific approach to existence. Although demons are immortals by nature, they can be destroyed with the necessary courage and strength. Demons are brutal, obsessive and ruthless creatures whose only objective is to kill and destroy. The most feared are without a doubt the intelligent demons who have learned the art of deception and can only be defeated by an unblemished and alert spirit.

Los servidores del Maligno son engendros detestables cuya sola visión resulta espantosa. Si bien los demonios son inmortales por naturaleza, pueden llegar a ser destruidos si se posee la valentía y la fuerza necesarias. Los demonios son criaturas brutales, obsesivas y despiadadas cuyo único objetivo es matar y destruir, pero los más peligrosos son sin duda los demonios inteligentes, que han desarrollado el arte del engaño y que sólo pueden ser vencidos por un espíritu limpio y despierto.

I servitori del Maligno sono essere detestabili e spaventosi alla vista. Anche se i demoni sono immortali per loro natura, possono essere sconfitti se si hanno il coraggio e la forza necessari. I demoni sono creature brutali, ossessive e spietate il cui unico obiettivo è uccidere e distruggere; i più pericolosi sono senza dubbio i demoni intelligenti che hanno sviluppato l'arte dell'inganno e possono essere sconfitti solo da uno spirito puro e vigile.

Os servidores do Maligno são criaturas horríveis que assustam só de olhar para eles. Embora os demónios sejam imortais por natureza, podem chegar a ser destruídos caso se possuam a coragem e a força necessárias. Os demónios são criaturas brutas, obcecadas e cruéis cujo único objectivo é matar e destruir, mas os mais perigosos são sem dúvica os demónios inteligentes, que desenvolveram a arte de enganar e só podem ser vencidos por um espírito limpo e atento.

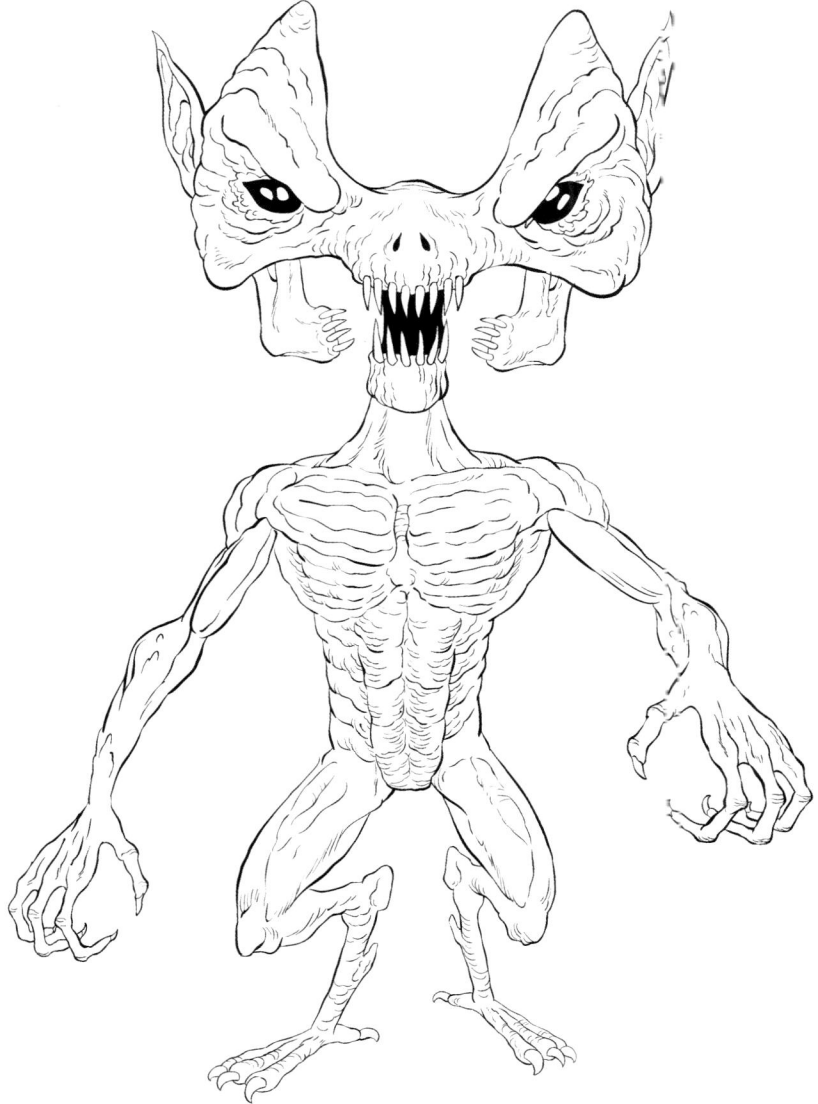

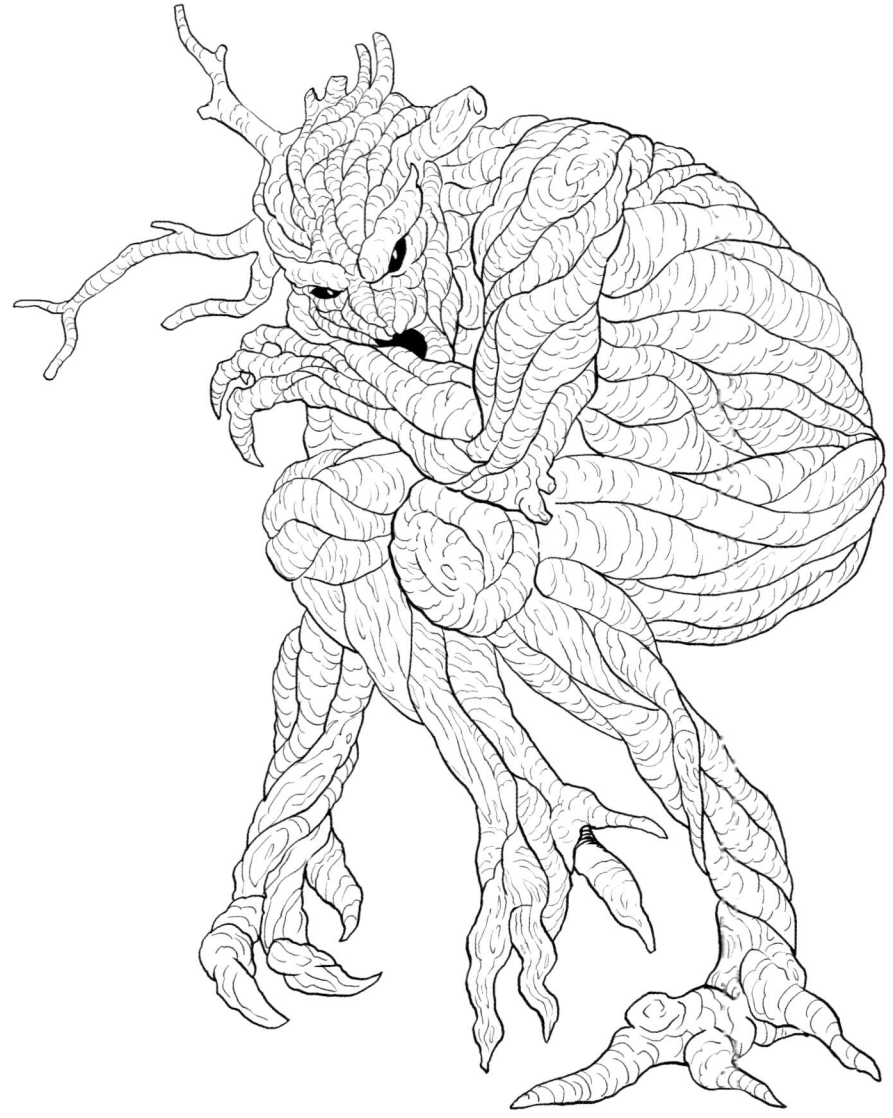

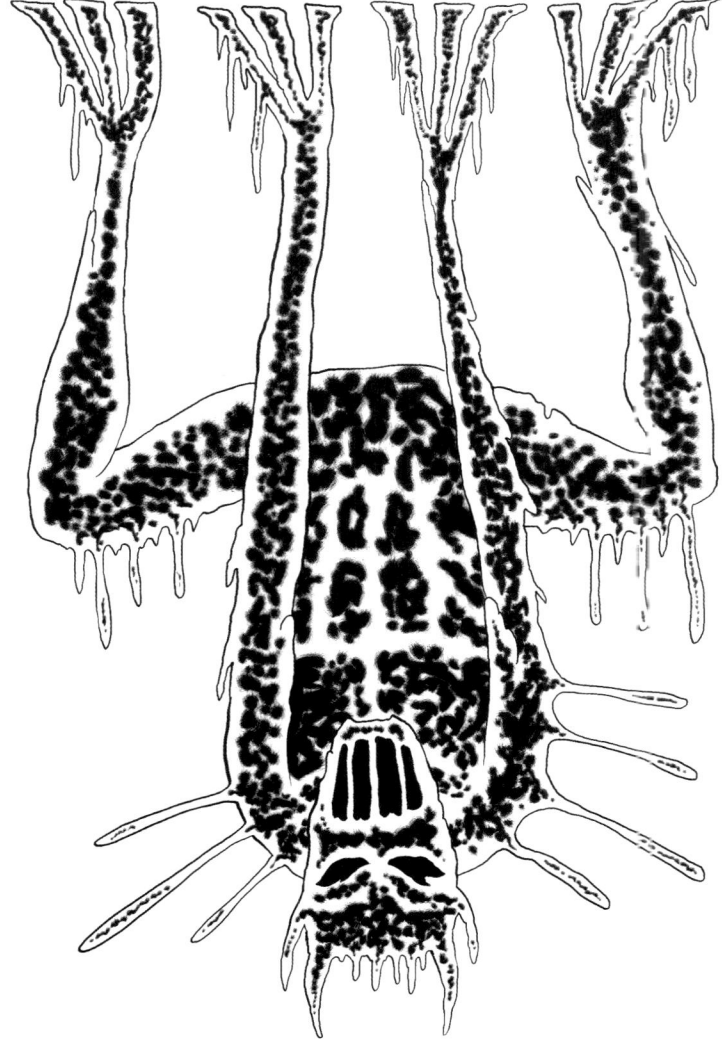

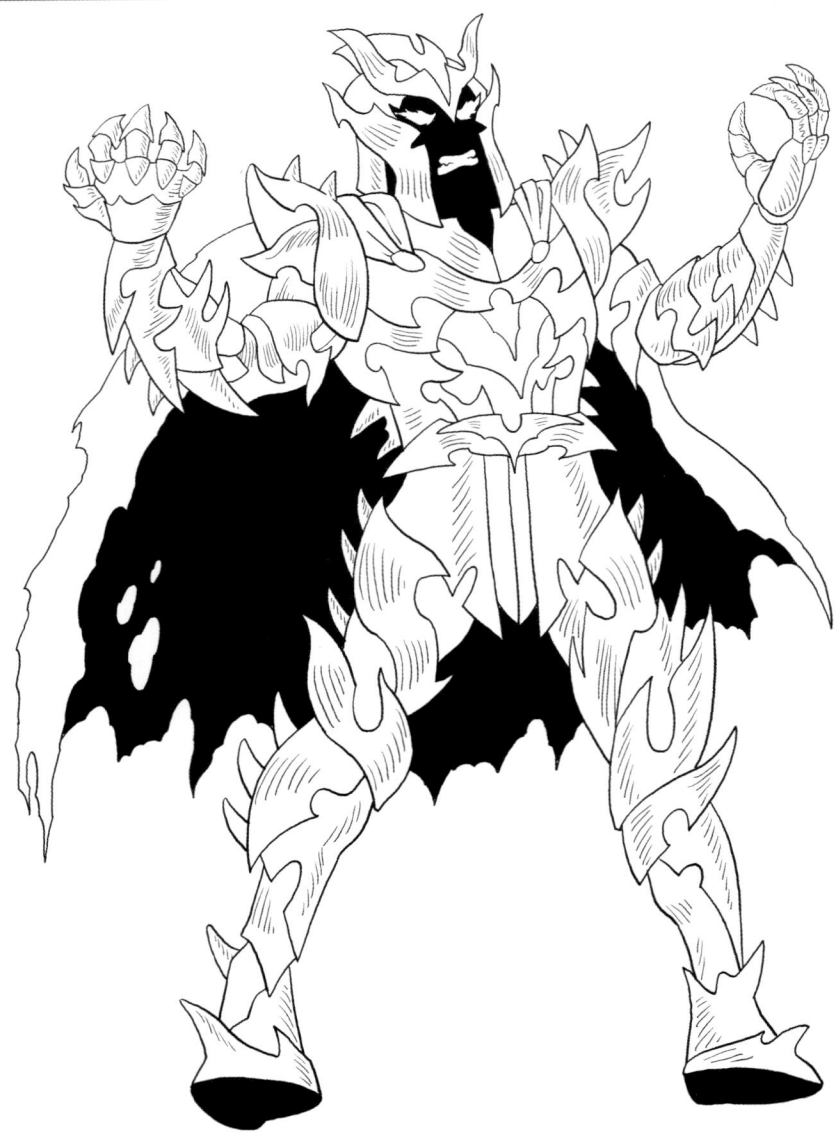

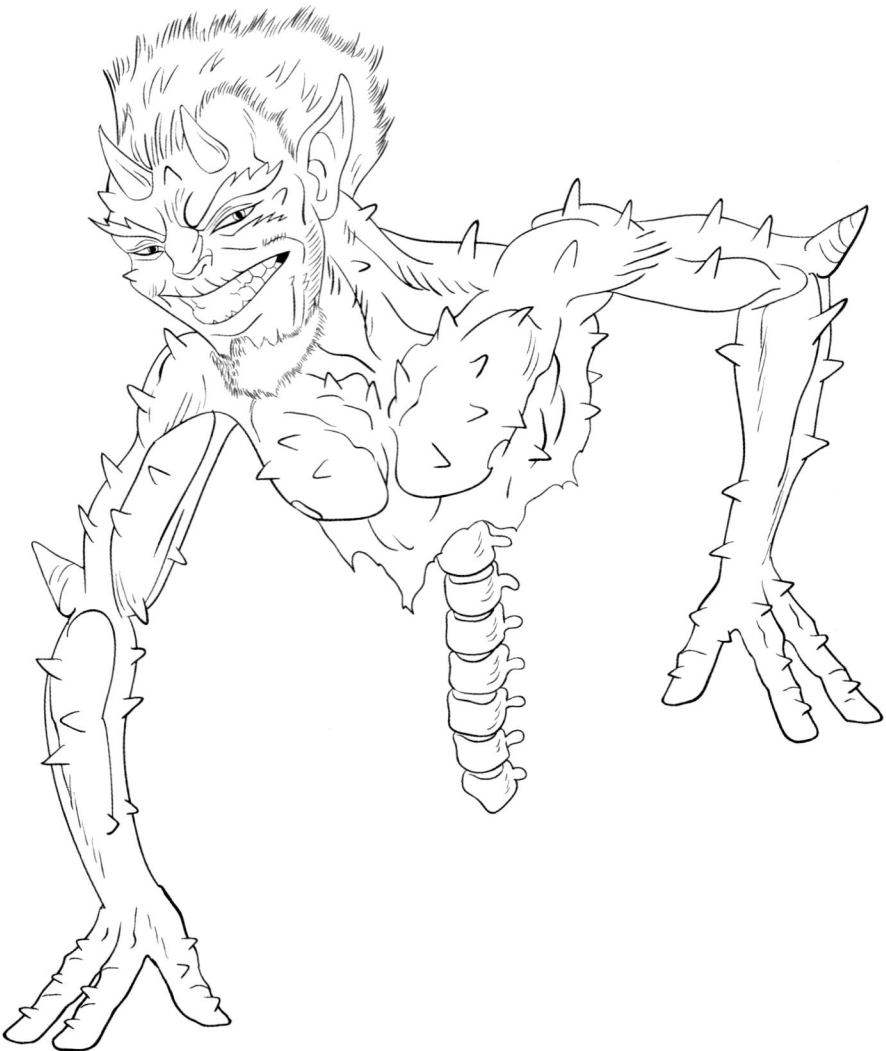

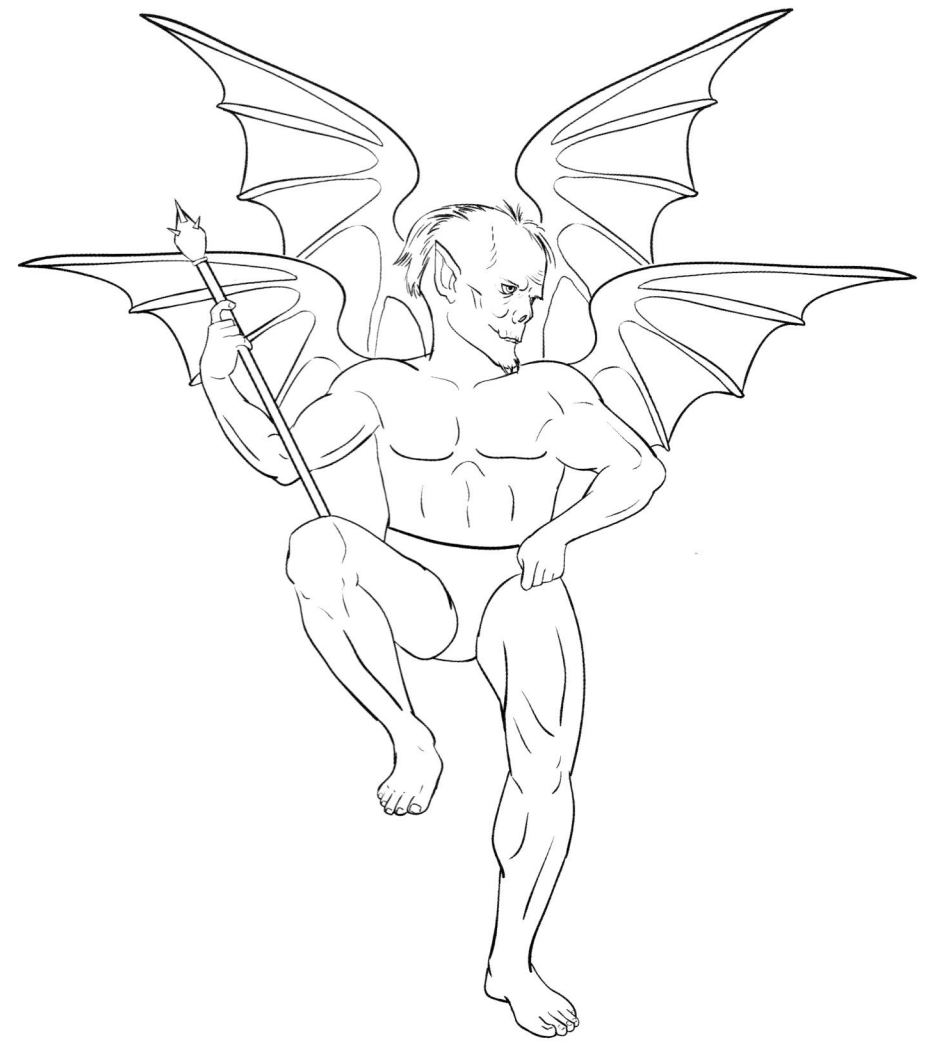

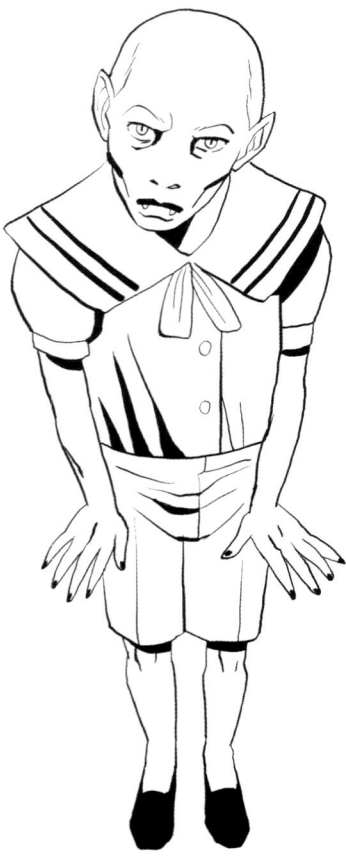

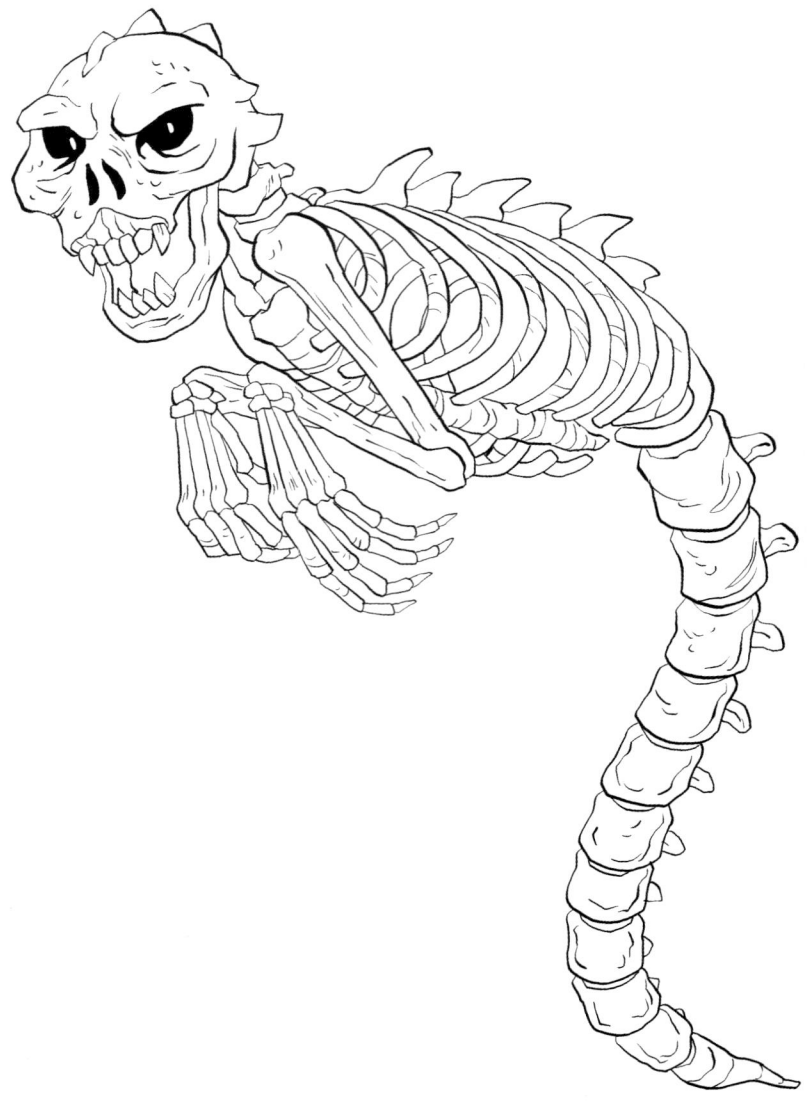

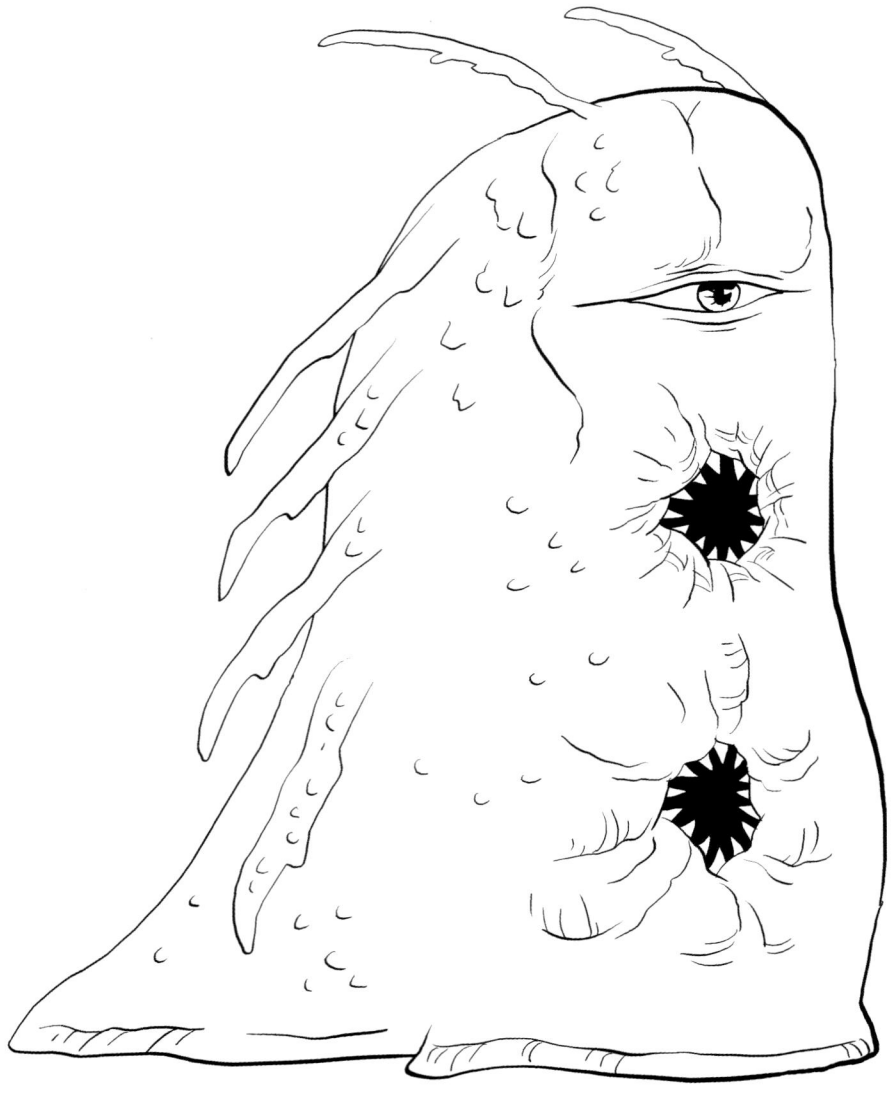

Magical beings
Seres mágicos
Esseri magici
Seres mágicos

Magicians, fairies, goblins, witches and oracles are all beings with very different natures, capable of performing supernatural wonders that defy the laws of the universe. Magicians are in touch with incomprehensible universal powers and take sides with the beings from which their powers emerge, defending the good or serving evil. Magical beings are feared and respected by their friends and enemies alike, and they are ruled by a strict code of conduct, a legacy from their ancestors.

Magos, Hadas, Duendes, Brujas y Oráculos son entidades de muy distinta naturaleza, capaces de realizar portentos sobrenaturales que desafían las leyes de nuestro universo. En contacto con incomprensibles fuerzas universales, los Seres Mágicos toman partido por las entidades de las que surgen sus poderes, defendiendo el bien o sirviendo al mal. Los Seres Mágicos son temidos y respetados tanto por amigos como por enemigos, y se rigen por un estricto código de conducta heredado de sus antecesores.

Maghi, Fate, Folletti, Streghe e Oracoli sono entità di natura molto diversa, capaci di magie soprannaturali che sfidano le leggi del nostro universo. Gli Esseri magici, che sono in contatto con incomprensibili forze universali, sostengono le entità dalle quali proviene il loro potere, difendendo il bene o servendo il male. Gli Esseri magici sono temuti e rispettati da amici e nemici e seguono un severo codice di condotta ereditato dai loro predecessori.

Feiticeiros, Fadas, Duendes, Bruxas e Oráculos são entidades de naturezas muito diferentes, capazes de realizar prodígios sobrenaturais que desafiam as leis do nosso universo. Em contacto com forças universais incompreensíveis, os Seres Mágicos ficam do lado das entidades das quais provêm os seus poderes, defendendo o bem ou servindo o mal. Os Seres Mágicos são temidos e respeitados tanto pelos seus amigos como pelos seus inimigos e regem-se por um rígido código de conduta herdado dos seus antecessores.

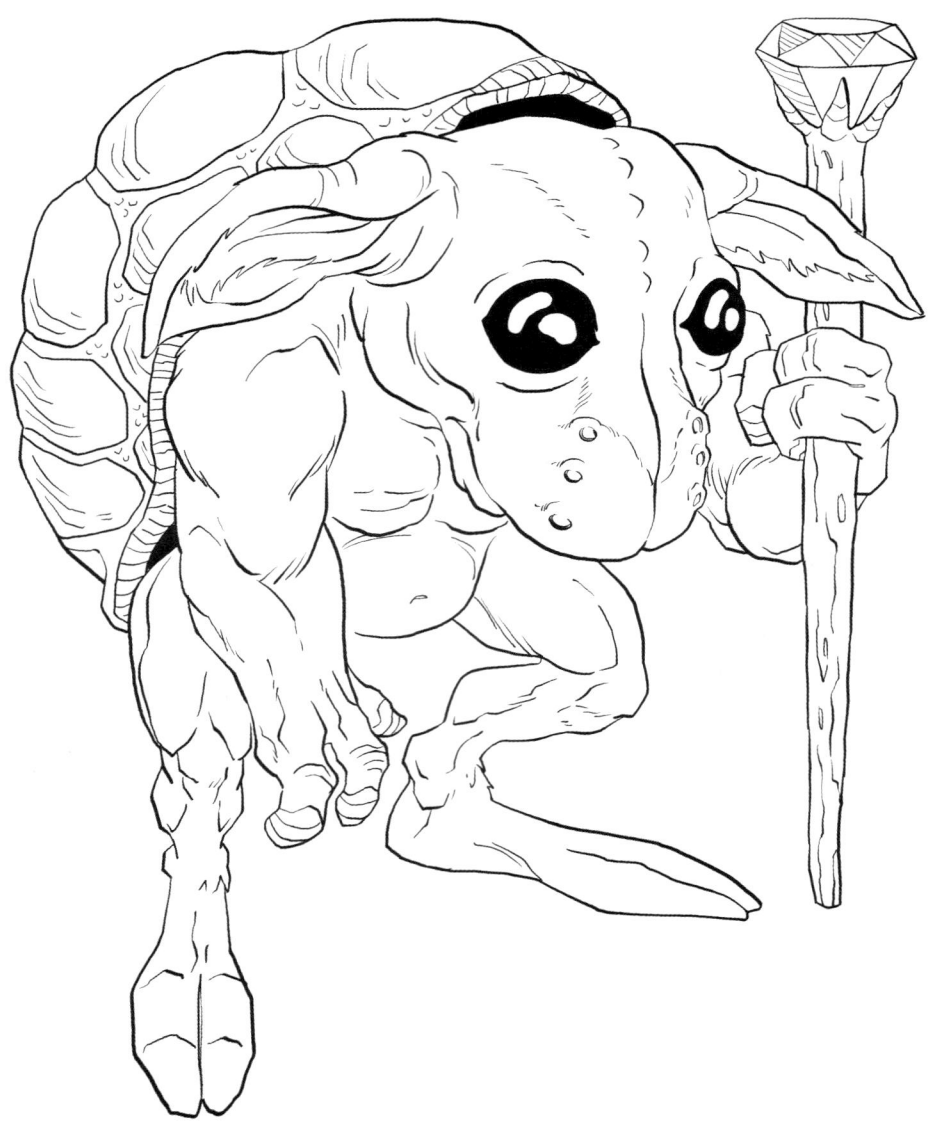

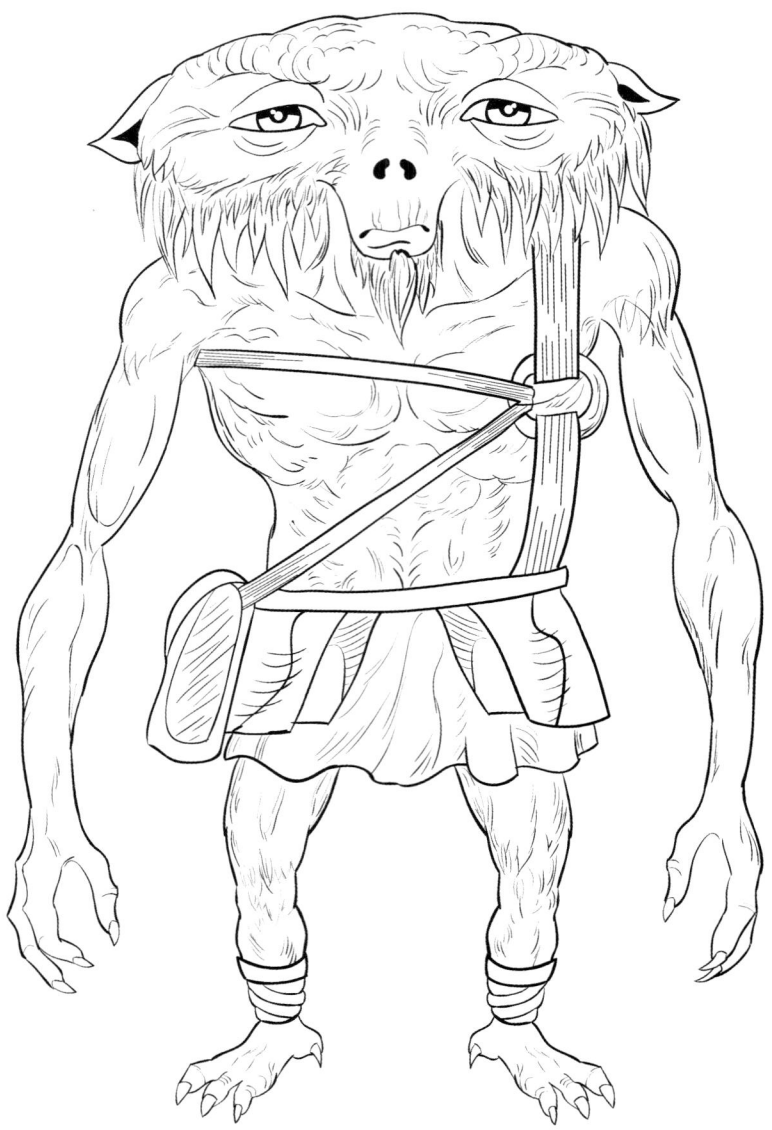

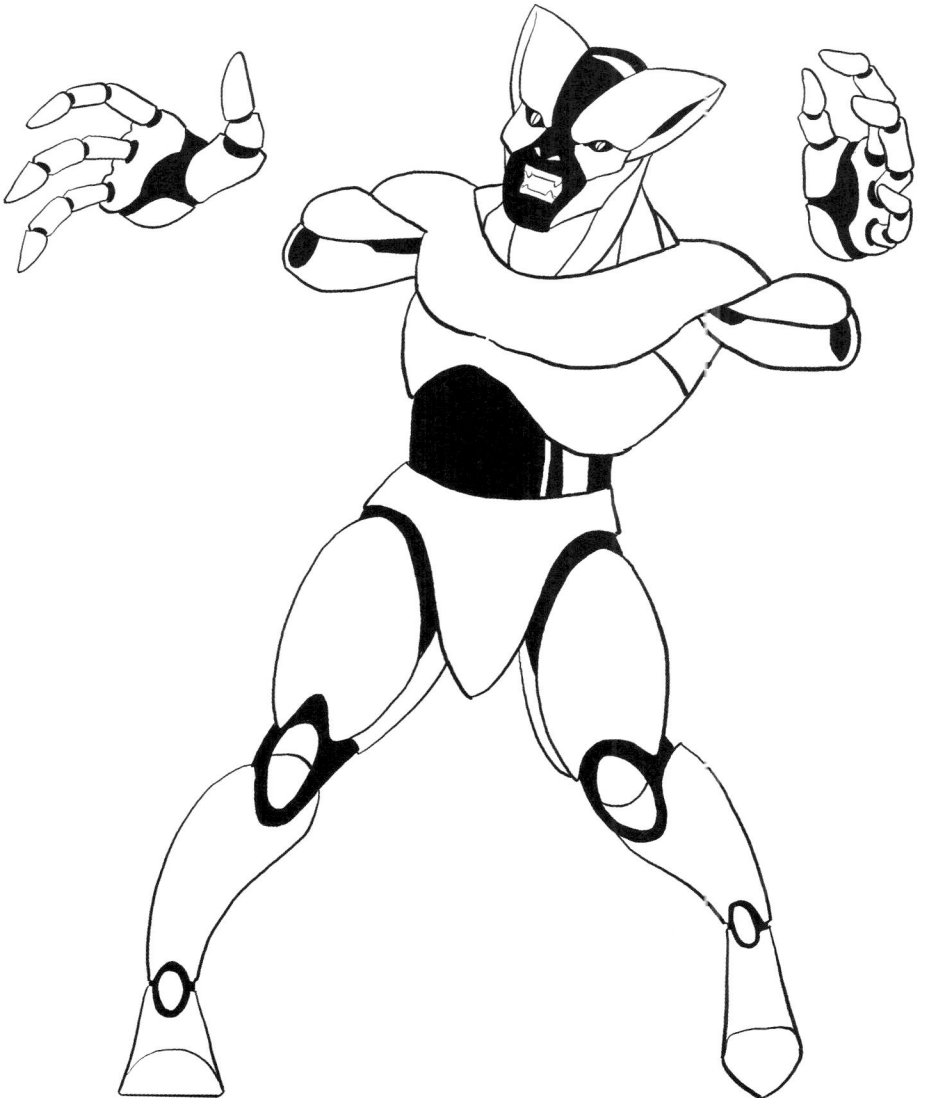

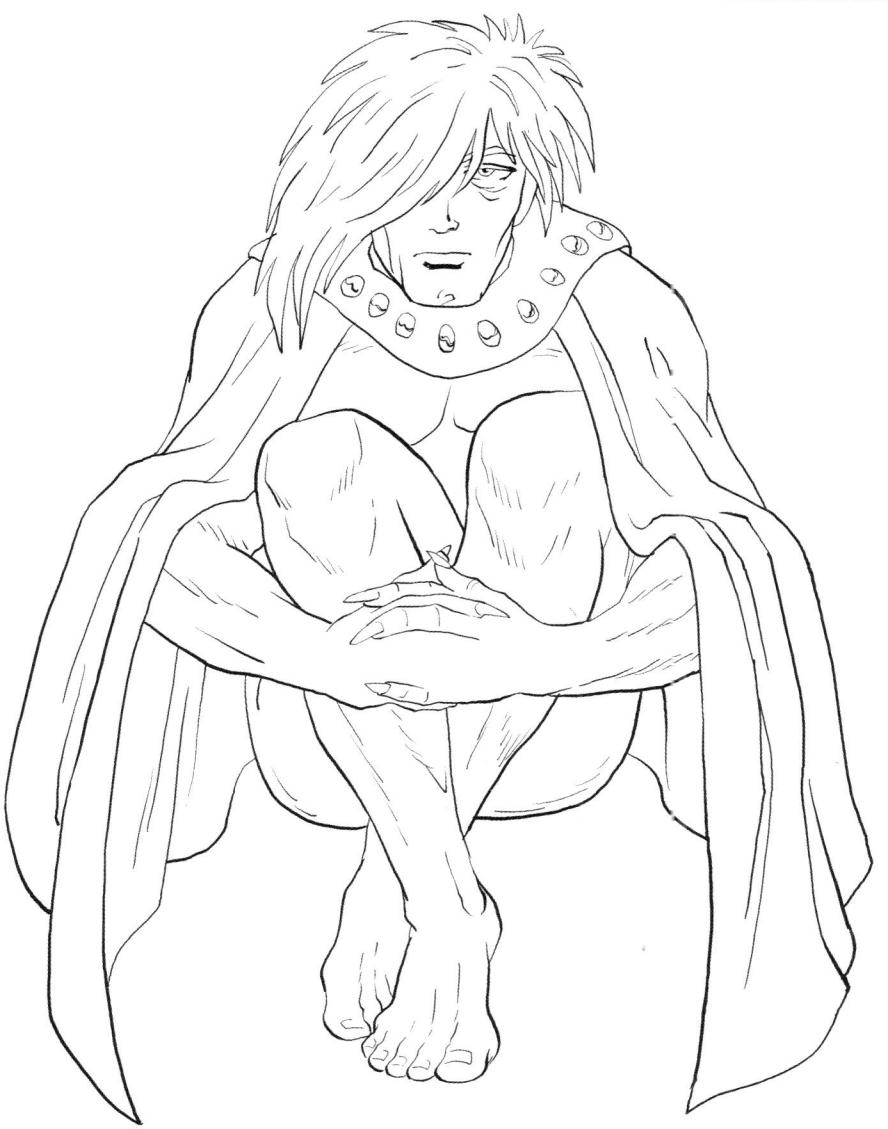

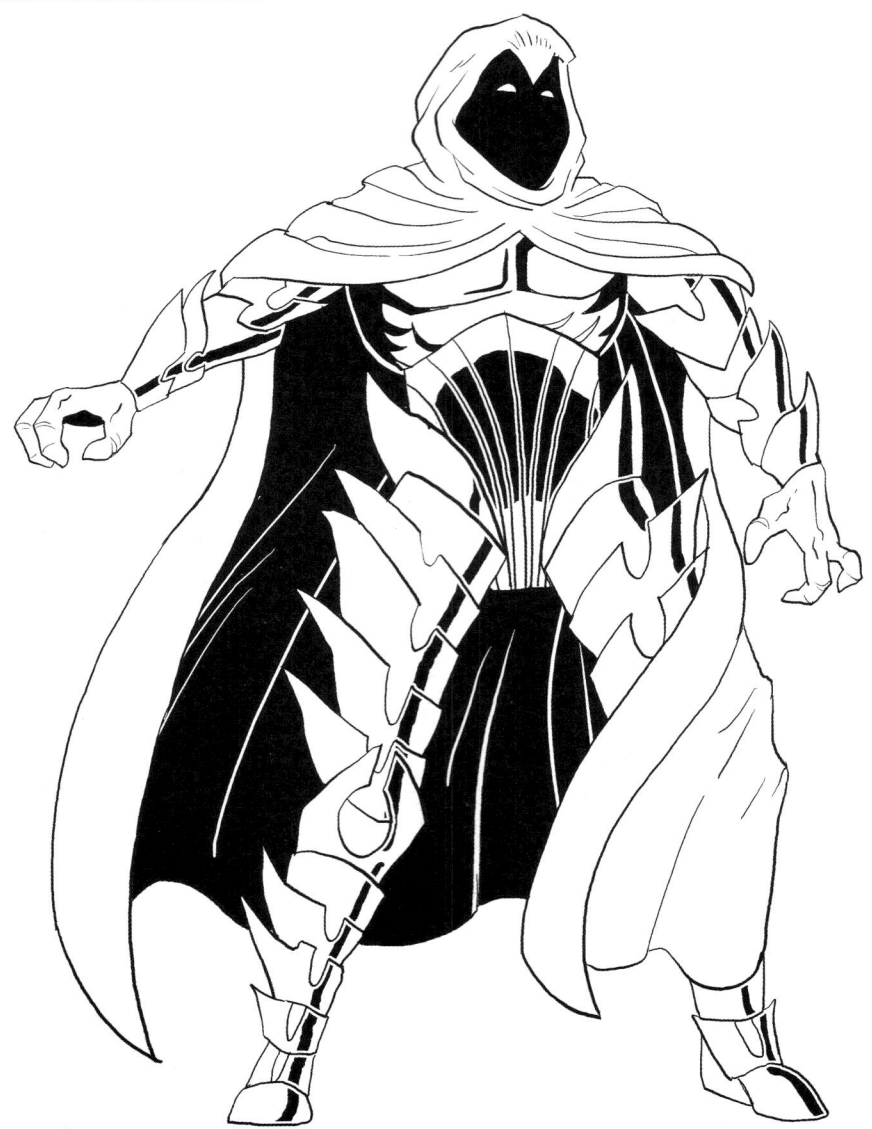

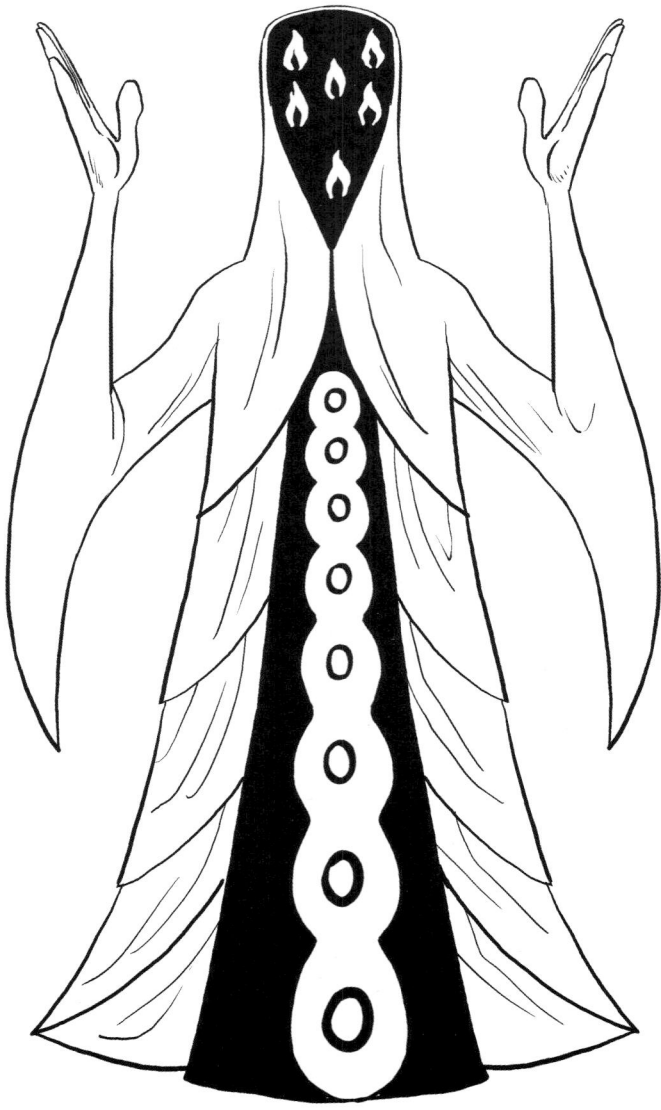

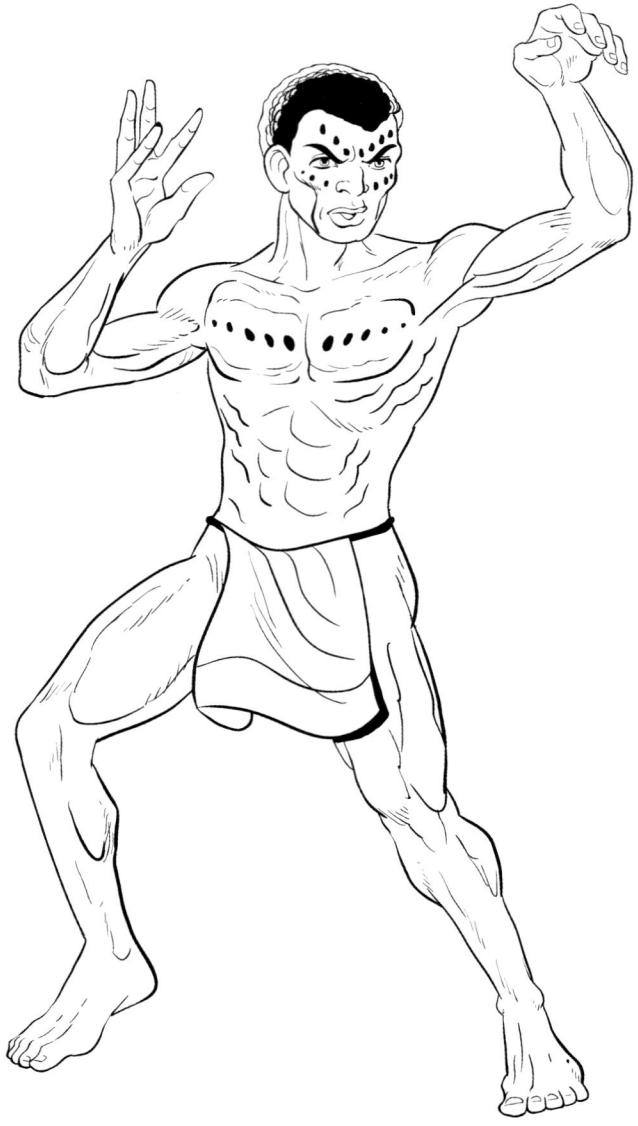

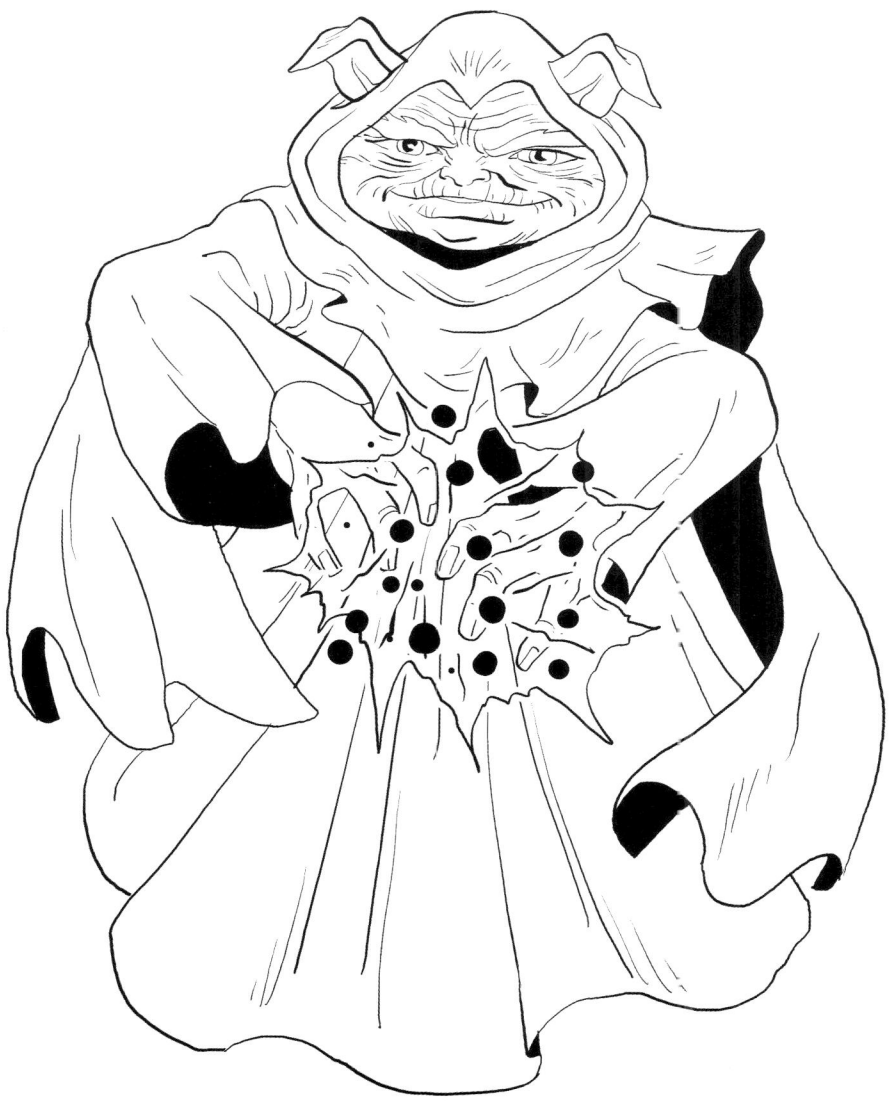

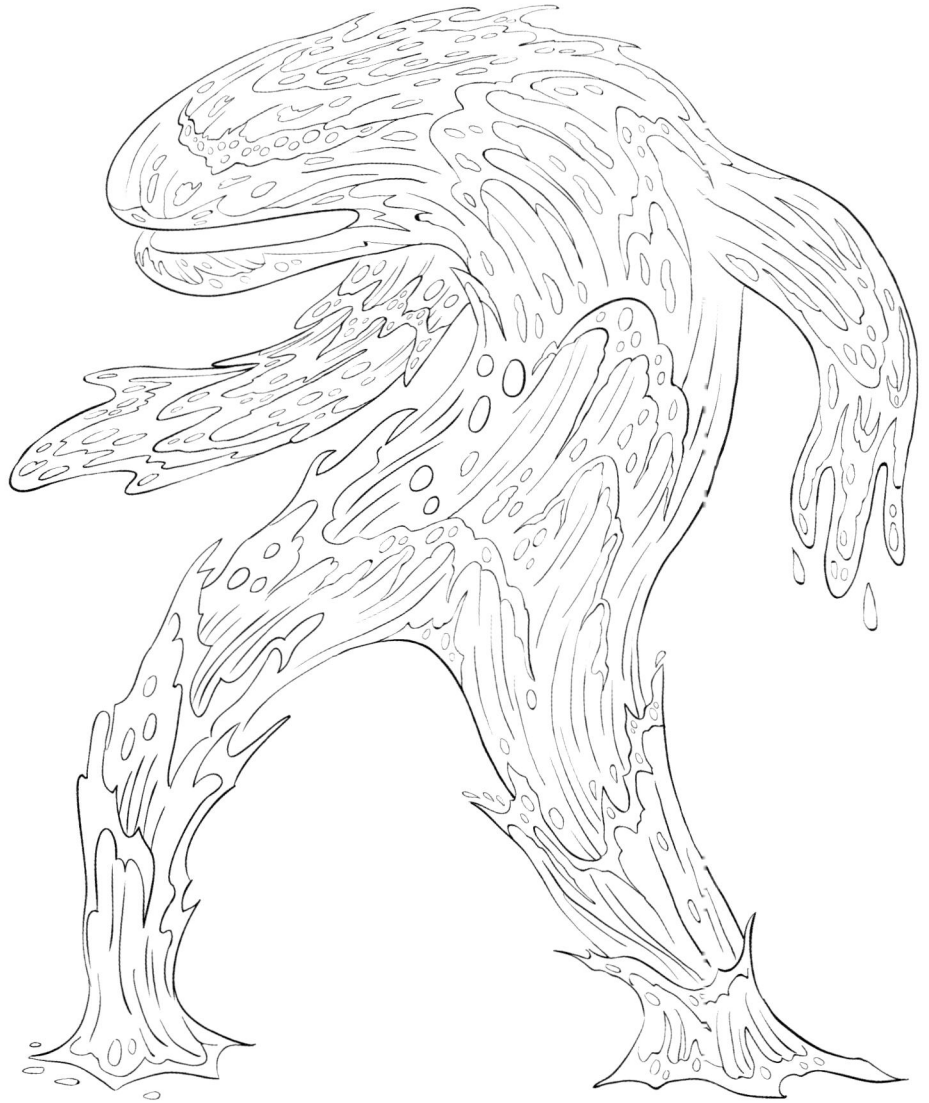

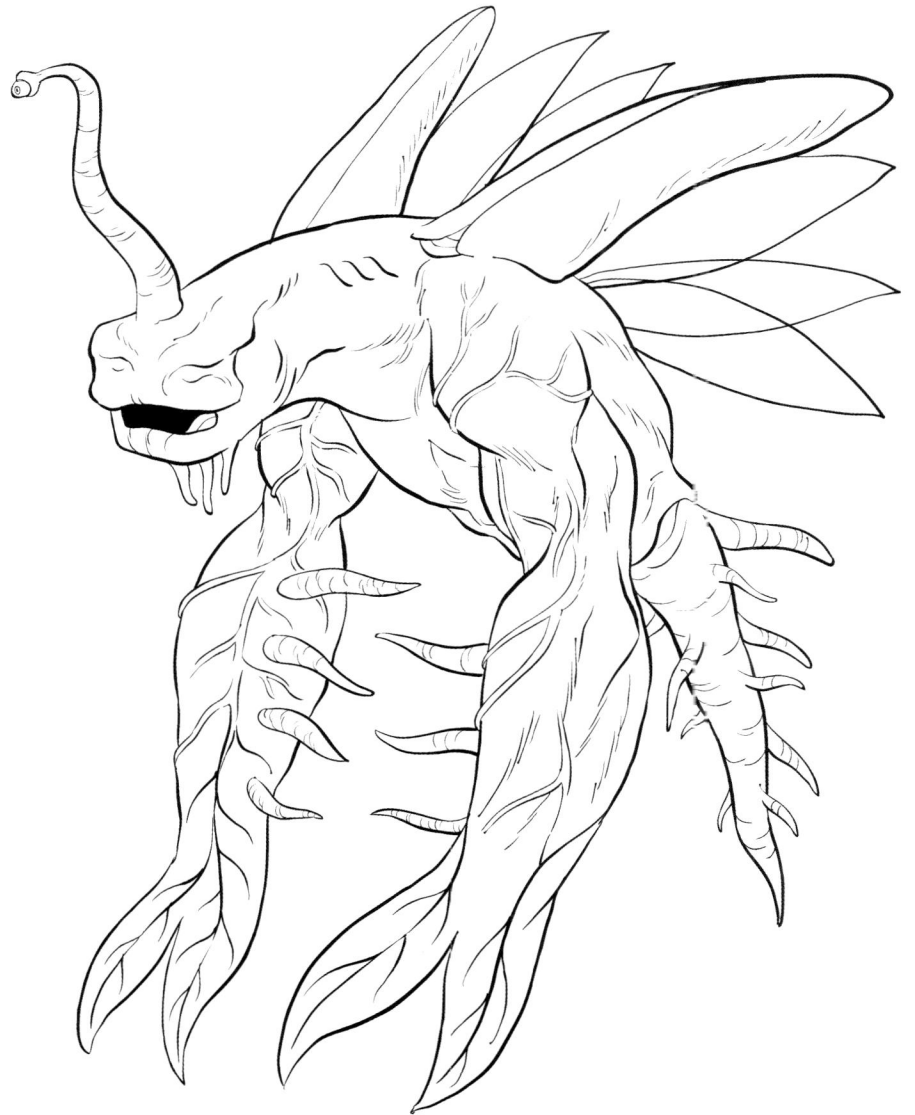